# The 5 Levels of CONSCIENCE

## The 5 Levels of CONSCIENCE

| Level | Archetype | Need | Emotions (To Self / To Creation / To Others) | | | Impulse | Manifestation |
|---|---|---|---|---|---|---|---|
| 5 | THE ARTIST | ENJOYMENT | JOY | EMPOWERMENT | LOVE | IMPULSE TO PLAY | ABUNDANCE |
| | | | **FULFILLMENT** | | | | |
| 4 | THE EMPATH | CONNECTION | PEACE | FAITH | COMPASSION | IMPULSE TO DO GOOD | POSITIVITY |
| | | | **HUMILITY** | | | | |
| 3 | THE CRITIC | VALIDATION | SHAME | ENTITLEMENT | ARROGANCE | IMPULSE TO JUDGE | ISOLATION |
| | | | **GRATITUDE** | | | | |
| 2 | THE EGOTIST | IMPACT | DESPAIR | HATRED | ENVY | IMPULSE TO HARM | SABOTAGE |
| | | | **ACCEPTANCE** | | | | |
| 1 | THE NARCISSIST | SECURITY | FEAR | FRUSTRATION | GREED | IMPULSE TO CONTROL | MANIPULATION |

If you'd like to test which level you have a tendency toward, go to 5levelsbook.com/quiz.

TITLE: The Five Levels of Conscience
By: Luis Ali
Edited by: Luis Ali
Copyright 2025

The author has made every effort possible to ensure the accuracy of the information presented in this book. However, the information herein is sold without warranty, either expressed or implied. Neither the author, publisher, nor any dealer or distributor of this book will be held liable for any damages caused, either directly or indirectly, by the instructions or information contained in this book. You are encouraged to seek professional advice before taking any action mentioned herein.

In accordance with the U.S. Copyright Act of 1976, the scanning, uploading, and electronic sharing of any part of this book without the permission of the publisher is unlawful piracy and theft of the author's intellectual property. If you would like to use material from this book (other than for review purposes), prior written permission can be obtained by contacting the author. Thank you for your support of the author's rights.

Notice of Rights: All rights reserved. No part of this book may be reproduced or transmitted in any form by any means, electronic, mechanical, photocopy, recording, or other without the prior and expressed, written permission of the author with the exception of brief cited quotes. Thank you for respecting the property rights of this and all authors.

Permission: For permission, reprints, excerpts, etc. contact:

Luis Ali at [Luis@5levelsbook.com](mailto:Luis@5levelsbook.com)
www.5LevelsBook.com
Instagram: @5levels.book
TikTok: @5levels.book
Mail: 3839 McKinney Ave #155-513, Dallas, TX 75204

# TABLE OF CONTENTS

| | |
|---|---|
| **INTRODUCTION** | **1** |
| **LEVEL 1 — THE NARCISSIST** | **15** |
| Level 1 Need: Security | 18 |
| Level 1 Connection to Self: Fear | 21 |
| Level 1 Connection to Creation: Frustration | 26 |
| Level 1 Connection to Others: Greed | 31 |
| Level 1 Impulse: The Impulse to Control | 36 |
| Level 1 Manifestation: Manipulation | 40 |
| **Level 1 Practice: Acceptance** | **48** |
| Level 1 Exercise | 51 |
| **LEVEL 2 — THE EGOIST** | **61** |
| Level 2 Need: Impact | 64 |
| Level 2 Connection to Self: Despair | 67 |
| Level 2 Connection to Creation: Hatred | 72 |
| Level 2 Connection to Others: Envy | 77 |
| Level 2 Impulse: The Impulse to Harm | 81 |
| Level 2 Manifestation: Sabotage | 85 |
| **Level 2 Practice: Gratitude** | **91** |
| Level 2 Exercise | 93 |
| **LEVEL 3 — THE CRITIC** | **103** |
| Level 3 Need: Validation | 106 |
| Level 3 Connection to Self: Shame | 109 |
| Level 3 Connection to Creation: Entitlement | 113 |
| Level 3 Connection to Others: Arrogance | 120 |
| Level 3 Impulse: The Impulse to Judge | 125 |
| Level 3 Manifestation: Isolation | 130 |
| **Level 3 Practice: Humility** | **133** |
| Level 3 Exercise | 136 |

## LEVEL 4 — THE EMPATH — 149

- Level 4 Need: Connection — 152
- Level 4 Connection to Self: Peace — 155
- Level 4 Connection to Creation: Faith — 159
- Level 4 Connection to Others: Compassion — 164
- Level 4 Impulse: The Impulse to do Good — 168
- Level 4 Manifestation: Positivity — 173
- **Level 4 Practice: Fulfillment** — **177**
    - Level 4 Exercise — 179

## LEVEL 5 — THE ARTIST — 191

- Level 5 Need: Enjoyment — 194
- Level 5 Connection to Self: Joy — 196
- Level 5 Connection to Creation: Empowerment — 200
- Level 5 Connection to Others: Love — 204
- Level 5 Impulse: Impulse to Play — 208
- Level 5 Manifestation: Abundance — 210
- **Level 5 Practice: Playfulness** — **213**

## CONCLUSION — 223

# INTRODUCTION

> "I don't want to be at the mercy of my emotions. I want to use them, to enjoy them, and to dominate them.
>
> — Oscar Wilde"

I, like you, have dealt with toxic emotions — both those that I have experienced within, and those that others have projected onto me. These toxic emotions, such as despair, greed, and envy, have led me and others to behave in ways that are not aligned with our well-being and, many times, in complete opposition to it. These emotions may have led us to say something that we later regretted, to cheat and lie unnecessarily, and to project rage and aggression onto complete strangers. We are all aware of this dynamic, and yet, we all continue to fall back into these negative patterns on a daily basis. This is something I've intrinsically felt and known since childhood, yet never felt I had the framework to consistently navigate. Nor did I even think there could *be* a simple way to navigate this chaos. I've always assumed that, as emotional creatures, we are all destined to exhibit destructive, emotional behaviors and there's nothing we can do about it. However, this perspective changed for me in a moment of lucidity that I feel was inspired by the divine, and one that I am excited to share with as many people as possible.

It all began in the most ordinary way. My girlfriend at the time had been invited to a family function in California while we were living in Texas. Although they had all come together for this celebration, there was tension and disharmony between them – traumas, unresolved issues, sibling and family rivalry, you name it. What made matters worse was that her family ranged from poor and middle-class to affluent people trying to assert financial superiority.

Sadly, my girlfriend's cousin used this opportunity that should have been reserved for reuniting with loved ones, catching up, and retelling old stories to make my girlfriend feel small and insignificant. They were around the same age, so her cousin made a big deal about how well she was doing in comparison to where she thought my girlfriend's life was at the time.

This woman's words left my girlfriend shaken and unsettled. She was so upset that she called me the next morning to vent her frustration with how her cousin made her feel. "I can't believe she would say something like that! .. and now we are going over to HER house today for lunch. I think I might just stay home."

I offered a word of comfort. "Well, you know the only reason she's saying these things is because she's judging you, and anybody who's judging you is judging themselves as well. She is simply projecting that judgment on to you." I did my best to encourage her and make her feel better. "She would never have said that if she didn't feel threatened by you in the first place."

We both knew that her cousin, in that particular moment, lacked compassion. But as my girlfriend and I spoke, I wondered why, if she knew that her cousin was wrong to behave that way, she couldn't just move past it. I wondered why she didn't choose to be grateful for all that she *did* have even if her cousin had more in one area. Yes, her cousin bore some responsibility. If she connected with her own humility and gratitude, she would likely feel compassion for those who have less than her instead of judgement. But what responsibility rested on my girlfriend's shoulders in the wake of the interaction? She didn't *want* to feel frustrated. She wanted to enjoy the short time she had with her family that she rarely sees, but she couldn't get past one rude interaction. If she had accepted that her cousin's words were her responsibility, she could have moved herself from frustration to joy. The solution seemed so simple when looking from the outside.

As I thought about this emotional dynamic, I asked myself for the first time: "Given that there is a simple and obvious solution for the emotions my girlfriend experienced in that moment, I wonder if any and all negative emotions have a simple solution? How incredible would that be?"

Most people can identify with the idea that we can survey our thoughts, words, and actions, tracking many of them back to our emotions. Out of those emotions arise impulses that influence how we behave and how our lives turn out. When we satisfy one of these impulses, it gives rise to momentary pleasure that will inevitably subside, like scratching an itch. The problem then becomes that, no matter how many times or to what great lengths we go to satisfy an impulse, or "scratch the itch", another emotion is bound to arise and, along with it, another impulse to satisfy. This can lead to destructive loops of chasing temporary pleasures and satisfactions, as opposed to building strong foundations of enduring happiness and fulfillment.

Most people can also identify with the idea that when we do realize we are feeling a particular emotion, we often don't know what to do with it. Internalize it or express it? Acknowledge it or ignore it? React to it or suppress it? Not to mention the internal dialogues that tell us we *should* feel these toxic emotions.

Fortunately, it turns out that there truly is a simple framework that we can turn to at any time and with any emotion that we want to release. In doing so, we can cleanse the old, toxic patterns of behavior that are caused by those emotions as simply as we cleanse our bodies in the shower.

*The 5 Levels of Conscience*

> Until you make the unconscious conscious, it will direct your life and you will call it fate.
>
> — C.G Jung

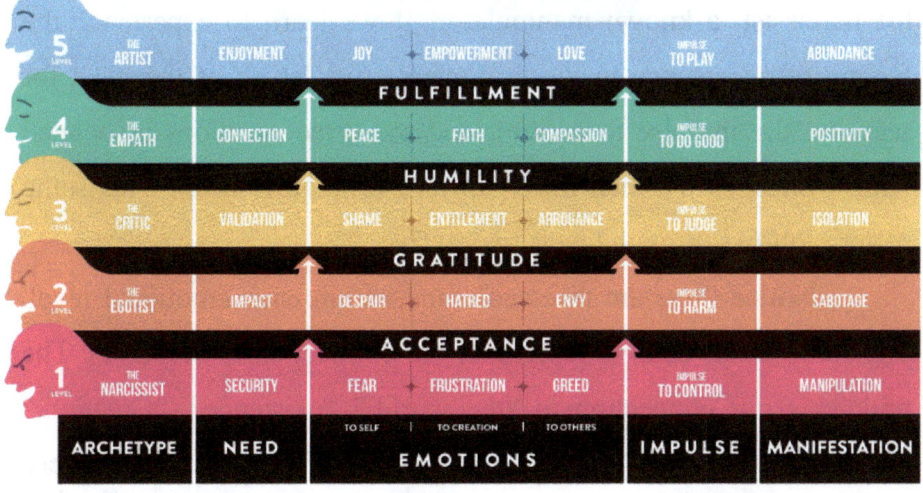

In the farthest left column is a list of archetypes to help you remember each level. Just to the right of each archetype is the underlying psychological need associated with that level. The three emotions that arise on each level are in the middle column. The column to the right of the emotions is the impulse that these emotions cause and in the furthest right column are the manifestations that happen in our lives as a result of giving into those impulses. Finally, between each level is the emotion we are missing that keeps us trapped in the level below it.

For example, level one contains the emotions of fear, frustration, and greed. We experience these emotions in a subconscious attempt to fulfill the psychological need for security and, as a result, we are compelled to control situations, outcomes, or other beings. When we give into the impulse to control, it manifests in our lives as manipulation. The archetype to remember this level is the narcissist, a known manipulator. If we learn to experience the feeling of acceptance in these moments, we let go of the need for security, the impulse to control, and the three emotions associated with level one. We then move upward to another level. This same pattern follows through levels two to five.

Notice there are three columns within each emotional level. The furthest left column represents our connection to ourselves. The middle is our connection to "the world," "existence," "Creation," "God," "the universe," or whatever else you prefer to call the forces of life beyond our control. For the remainder of this book, I will use the terms "Creator" and "Creation." The right column is our connection to others and how we show up in relationships.

These emotions are all connected, and you will likely feel the emotion that corresponds to the perspective you are taking. For example, if you are on level two, without gratitude, and your attention is focused on yourself, you will likely feel despair. If your attention then turns to others, you will likely feel envy.

You will also notice a tendency for the emotion you are feeling to transform into the one directly above it as you move past that level with the exercises. For example, fear may turn into despair as you accept the reality of a certain situation. Despair may turn into shame after you experience gratitude and regret the way you were behaving. Shame may turn into peace, or relief, as you forgive yourself for doing this. Relief then turns into joy as you make your way fully into the present moment, realizing there is no need to hold on to the situation.

You may have also noticed that anger and rage are not included in the framework. The reason for this is that all toxic emotions can lead to anger if they are not interrupted with healthier emotions. When one of these emotions begins to overwhelm us, we typically respond with rage. This is especially true if the emotion threatens our sense of self (ego), our safety, or the safety of those around us. Shame can turn into anger; frustration can turn into anger; envy can turn into anger. Any one of the emotions on the first three levels can turn into anger, so the prudent thing to do is to identify the root emotion of the anger and move past it that way. If you recognize you are feeling angry, try to trace that anger back to a deeper emotion. Ask yourself, "What am I angry about?" then a layer deeper, "Why does that bother me?" and so forth until you can recognize the emotions beneath the surface. That being said, anger tends to create an impulse to harm, and gratitude is always the best way to move past that immediate impulse.

## USING THE CHART

We can use the chart by consciously noting any emotion we are feeling in the moment, any impulse we are having in the moment, or any life manifestation we are experiencing in any moment or over time. Once we've realized we are operating on a certain level, then we can move up the chart using the solution emotion just above that level. If you know you are upset but can't seem to figure out which level you are on, it is generally easiest to reflect on what your emotions are making you want to do. Follow that back to the impulses on the chart and then to the corresponding emotions.

As you learn the framework and practice moving through it, it is important that you do not identify with any particular level. Avoid saying things like, "I am on level one and, therefore, I am a narcissist." or, "You are such a narcissist!" It is much healthier to say things like, "My inner narcissist has been activated." or "You are being *the* narcissist right now."

Even if we are experiencing the emotions and the impulses from level one, they do not define who we are. We have simply been triggered at that time and with regard to that specific situation or relationship. When we are at home, we might be on level four. Then, while we're at work, we might experience impulses from level three.

## The 5 Levels of Conscience

When we go to lunch with a friend, we might move to another level. We may only be on a certain level for a few minutes, or it could last days. One situation might trigger certain emotions one day and that same situation triggers completely different emotions the next day. This is all okay. Emotional mastery is a process and not a destination.

Sometimes, you may find that you move rather swiftly from one level to the next. Other times, the progression may feel slower and more labored. Sometimes, you will move directly from a lower level to level five with just one exercise, and other times, you will need to remove the blockages on each level one by one.

Be patient with yourself as you *will* be challenged by your inner resistance as you attempt to move up the chart using the exercises I will provide. When a toxic emotion is particularly intense, it will compel you to stay inside that emotion with the message that you *should* feel that way, and you don't want to feel differently. This is actually a great indicator that you are on the right path. The greater the resistance the better. This is because, once you break through, you will achieve the most meaningful and lasting changes. As Rumi says: "The cure for pain is in the pain." You can either move past that resistance consciously, patiently, and willfully, or you can sit with and experience the emotions long enough for their intensity to dissipate. In these moments, it helps to "come to your senses," noting one or two things you can see, hear, and touch while you breathe slowly and intentionally. This will bring you out of your mind and into the moment, which will turn down the volume of your inner dialogue.

The most important part of practicing the exercises is to concentrate on *feeling* the solution emotion as deeply as you can. Don't focus on the outcome you want to achieve, the situation or person that inspired the negative state, or anything else except the moment you are in, the action you are performing, and feeling the desired "solution" emotion. If you are not experiencing emotional resistance, but are still struggling to feel the solution emotion, it's likely because you are blocked on one of the lower levels. Start from the beginning of the chart and work your way back up. You also don't have to feel a negative emotion or recognize toxic impulses and manifestations to practice. You can make it a daily practice to do any one or even all of the exercises to prevent these patterns from arising in the first place.

Before we dive more deeply into the framework, it is important to note that, as humans, we move between narcissism and altruism on a regular basis—narcissism being a self-centeredness that lacks empathy for others and altruism being a perspective that incorporates the highest good for all. Every one of us can find ourselves experiencing the emotions and impulses of either extreme. At the bottom of the diagram are the emotions and behaviors that are the most self-serving. They are centered around our urge toward self-preservation, which pulls our awareness away from others and into ourselves.

As we move up the scale, our energy and awareness both expand toward altruism. Once we reach the top, the concerns for ourselves and others are aligned. Just before the top, this level of altruism feels like the highest because it transforms our focus from completely inward to completely outward. After all, what could be higher? Altruism is selfless concern for the well-being and welfare of others. Right? When we are being most altruistic, we prioritize the needs and interests of others, often putting them above our own, don't we? It involves acts of generosity, charity, and self-sacrifice... Or does it?

Despite what it seems at first glance, this type of altruism is not the highest state of conscience. While it involves selflessness, it can often morph in a complete disregard for one's own well-being. This can lead to deep-seated resentment toward others, and a deterioration of health that is hard to fix because, conceptually, we believe we are doing the highest good. This level is characterized by the desire to do good for others; however, there's still that *striving to change things*, even though the goal is change for the better. There is nothing wrong with wanting to change things and making a concerted effort to do so. However, this "wanting" and "striving" to change can easily become pathological and destructive if attached to, and fueled by, toxic emotions and behavior patterns. This is also true if it is regarding circumstances, situations, or attributes that we fundamentally cannot change.

The highest level of conscience we can achieve is when there is no desire to change anything at all. It's just an impulse to enjoy the world with others and to be present and joyous in the moment. Our desires and the desires of others are no longer in the picture. All that matters is sharing the joyous present moment with the people around us.

Think about the first time you held a newborn baby or a time when you were completely immersed in a sport or activity that you love. Think about a time when you treated yourself to a walk through the forest to simply enjoy nature or a time when you were locked in a passionate embrace with the one you love after time apart. These are occasions when we are fully immersed in the present moment and not seeking to change ourselves, to change someone else, or to be altruistic. We are simply basking in the light of Creation and the beauty of the now.

The disruptive emotions we feel from time to time can be thought of as messages from our Creator that require us to integrate certain perspectives in order for us to reach these states of fulfillment. We've all felt a moment of inspiration where things seemingly "click," and we release some toxic thought pattern as we go into a state of effortless flow. These are moments where we have overcome some emotional block, or message, by shifting our perspective. Refusing to integrate these perspectives and process these emotions is when we sink into toxic behaviors and, eventually, madness. This book will give you the tools to integrate these messages quickly and efficiently while limiting toxic outbursts.

Using this framework you can learn to recognize the patterns, identify where you are, and consistently move past them in a matter of minutes. The goal is to move more often to the state of pure contentment where nothing needs to be changed. Sometimes, just the awareness of the phenomena will be enough for the toxic emotions and impulses to dissipate. Other times, it will take an active approach. In the following chapters, I'll illustrate very simple exercises to accomplish this.

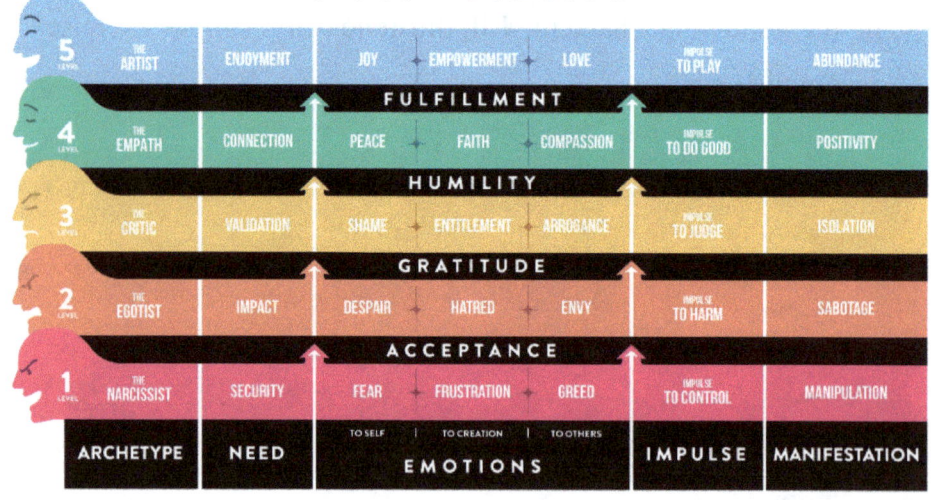

*The 5 Levels of Conscience*

# LEVEL 1
# THE NARCISSIST

In 1776, Benjamin Franklin was sent to France as a diplomat for the American colonies. His mission was clear: secure French support for the Revolutionary War. Though Franklin was a master of persuasion, the stakes were high. The colonies were struggling, and without French aid, the war effort seemed doomed.

Franklin adopted a carefully calculated strategy. He flattered French aristocrats, attended lavish parties, and won over many admirers with his charm. Franklin did everything he could to steer conversations toward the grandeur of the American cause and away from any doubts about its viability. However, French officials remained hesitant, unwilling to fully commit their resources to a precarious rebellion.

As weeks turned to months, Franklin began to see his approach backfiring. His attempts to manipulate the narrative created divisions within the American delegation, and French ministers grew wary of his intentions.

In a moment of clarity, Franklin resolved to change his approach. He stopped trying to steer every conversation and instead focused on embodying the ideals of the American cause—simplicity, honesty, and resilience. He spent his evenings sharing humble anecdotes of colonial life and the principles of liberty. He allowed the French to reach their own conclusions rather than pressing them for immediate support.

Over time, his authenticity won trust. France eventually pledged its resources to the war, a decision that helped secure American independence.

Franklin's story is a reminder that true influence arises not from control, but from faith in our values and patience in their expression. By letting go of his fears and manipulations, Franklin achieved more than he ever could through forceful persuasion.

# THE NARCISSIST

> The main condition for the achievement of love is the overcoming of one's narcissism. The narcissistic orientation is one in which one experiences as real only that which exists within oneself, while the phenomena in the outside world have no reality in themselves but are experienced only from the viewpoint of their being useful or dangerous to oneself. The opposite pole to narcissism is objectivity; it is the faculty to see other people and things as they are, objectively, and to be able to separate this objective picture from a picture which is formed by one's desires and fears.
>
> — Erich Fromm

## The 5 Levels of Conscience

The archetype of level one is the narcissist. In Greek mythology, Narcissus destroys himself as he falls in love with his own image reflected in the water. This represents an endless loop of self-interest that causes the afflicted person to lose sight of everything in life outside of their own desires, stifling the ability to love anyone or anything else. When we are being narcissistic, we generally have a need for excessive admiration, power, and control. We will manipulate with little to no empathy, treating others as if they are mere objects. We will completely disregard the well-being of others outside of ourselves and sometimes those in our immediate concern, given that it benefits us in some way. We may even feel a twisted sense of satisfaction when we are able to successfully manipulate or exert control over others. It is important to note that Narcissus falls in love with his *reflected image*, not with himself. This represents the image of ourselves we create and obsess over in our minds, not our true selves. Please also keep in mind that we all exhibit narcissistic tendencies and there is no need to condemn ourselves for that.

Level-one behavior is rooted in a misguided or overwhelming need for security that then triggers the emotions of fear, frustration, and greed. In this chapter, we will cover the dynamics of this phenomenon, the effects, and how you will know if you are being motivated by it. At the end of this chapter, and every chapter, I will provide you with a simple exercise you can do to move upward from this level. If, at any point, you realize you are experiencing the symptoms of what you are reading, I encourage you to skip to the exercise at the end of that chapter, practice for a few minutes, and come back to the section you were reading.

The emotions of this level, as well as those from levels two and three, lend themselves to rumination, which is the repetition of negative thought patterns. This can keep us permanently trapped without ever experiencing higher-level emotions until we learn how to properly release them.

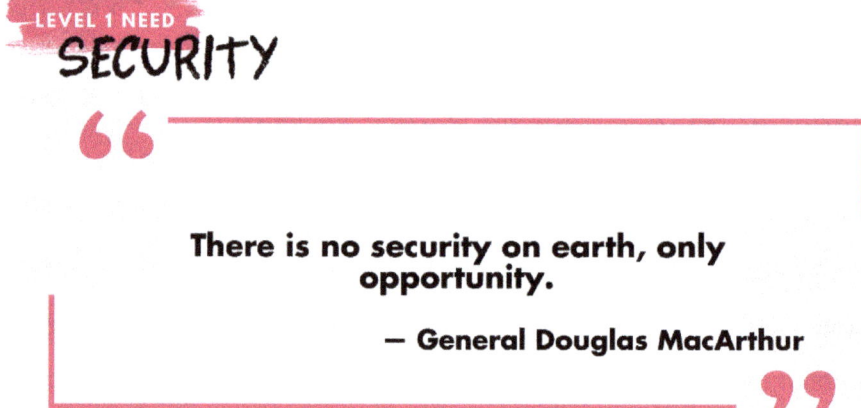

## LEVEL 1 NEED
# SECURITY

> "There is no security on earth, only opportunity."
>
> — General Douglas MacArthur

Very deeply rooted in our biology is a psychological need for safety and security. The world is a dangerous place, and nature is unapologetically ruthless. There is no doubt that our ancestors who prioritized safety and security increased their chances of living long enough to pass on their genetics. This wired our brains to effectively identify and avoid threats. It is impossible for us to move on to other needs and wants if our lives are at stake. Can you imagine taking a break from being chased by a lion to have a snack? This is why level one emotions will always be a relevant part of our experience, although one that requires understanding and adaptation since the majority of existential threats we once faced are now gone.

It is perfectly normal for us to take precautionary measures, such as locking our doors, withholding sensitive information, and scanning our surroundings for potential threats. All of these can be done with a calm sense of acceptance that we cannot ultimately know of, nor prevent all harmful occurrences. In addition, some occurrences that appear harmful at first may actually be beneficial from another perspective. The toxic pathology of level one begins when this need for security is misguided or overwhelming. In this scenario, no matter how many precautionary measures we take, we never actually feel secure.

As opposed to physical, existential threats, our desire for security could turn toward desired outcomes, opinions, and situations that pose no real harm to us. This could be things like the security we feel we gain in planning every single word of an important conversation. Or maybe it is cheating at a game to ensure victory. It could be excluding certain people in gatherings or conversations that we believe threaten our desired goals. Perhaps you are a concerned parent who refuses to let your children be exposed to thoughts or ideas that you do not agree with. Sometimes we avoid telling someone a truth because we fear the consequences. Maybe we refuse to spend money on things that make us happy and on the people that we love because we feel we need to have a certain dollar amount in our bank account to feel secure in our opinion of ourselves.

Many of us at times will also have trouble enjoying the moment because this need for safety and security has permeated nearly every thought and perception we entertain. We reject any new activity, person, or place because the unknown poses threats that we have not come across. Better the devil you know than the one you don't. When this happens, it is common for us to seek out and absorb as much information as we can, often becoming obsessive. This constant anxiety is no way to live a fulfilled life and can often result in panic attacks and paranoia.

Understanding our need for safety and security can be extremely helpful in recognizing level one behaviors. This allows us to distinguish what truly matters to us, and what is truly necessary for survival, from what may be holding us back from the fully enjoying the short time we have on earth. The distinguishing factor will be the emotions tied to the behavior. Sometimes it will be obvious, and other times, it will require a bit of self-reflection:

- "Am I doing this because it makes sense or because I am afraid, frustrated, or greedy?"

- "Am I trying to control anyone or anything about the situation?"

- "Is there any manipulation involved in what I am doing right now?"

- "Am I content to accept the outcome if my attempts fail?"

Once we understand the dynamics of our desire for safety, we can more easily distinguish between the behaviors that serve us and the ones that do not. In order to live a fulfilled life, we have to accept that life is unpredictable and that it is in our best interest to be confident in our ability to adapt. This is not to say that we should throw caution to the wind and put ourselves in dangerous situations that serve no benefit. We can easily live a safe and secure life that is also full of carefree joy by balancing and understanding our need for security.

# FEAR

> **Fear is the main source of superstition, and one of the main sources of cruelty. To conquer fear is the beginning of wisdom.**
> **— Bertrand Russell**

Fear is a powerful and primal emotion that arises in response to a perceived threat or danger that has compromised our psychological need for safety and security. In some cases, it is a natural instinct designed to protect us from harm and ensure our survival. Fear triggers a physiological and psychological response called the fight-or-flight response in the body which prepares us to confront the threat or run from it. Real physical processes happen when we are afraid like an increased heart rate, heightened senses, dilated pupils, and the release of stress hormones like adrenaline. This heightened state of awareness can help us perform at our best when we are in imminent danger and when it matters most.

However, fear can be paralyzing and limit our potential if it becomes compulsive, overwhelming, or irrational. When there is no real present danger during a fear trigger, we can experience trauma and begin to act in ways that are seemingly illogical from the outside. This can result from real or imagined threats and can manifest in different forms, including specific phobias, anxieties, or general feelings of unease. If these become prolonged, they can lead to the development of personality issues. For example, a deep-rooted fear of inadequacy or criticism could result in aversion to social interactions and a lack of social or relationship skills over time.

Fear underpins the entirety of level one. In frustration and greed, there is generally a fear of inadequacy or loss of livelihood beneath the surface. There could also be a fear of having to rely on others and a fear of loss of admiration or status. These emotions are designed to protect us from something we feel threatens our very existence. Our subconscious desires a sense of security and will encourage us to achieve that by any means necessary, including manipulation.

## The 5 Levels of Conscience

In this framework, fear also includes other similar emotions including:

- Anxiety
- Dread
- Insecurity
- Apprehension
- Trepidation
- Worry
- Unease
- Nervousness
- Panic
- Alarm
- Terror
- Fright
- Phobia
- Intimidation
- Concern

We often fear the unknown and feel uncomfortable when we are faced with uncertainty or unfamiliar situations. The fear of the unknown arises from the sense of security we believe we gain from predictability. We tend to fear what we don't understand or cannot control because that could result in an outcome that we believe is bad for us. Our instinct is then to search for the aspects of the scenario that we *can* control through force or manipulation. When we act on these, many times, we will stop at nothing and completely ignore ethics and morality because the fear response is telling us that our life is at stake. For example, someone may go to excessive or unethical lengths to learn information about someone they are dating because they believe having that predetermined knowledge will help them to portray themselves as a better potential match. Otherwise, they may die alone.

Fear can also be triggered by our past, where traumatic events or negative experiences have left scars on our psyche. These triggers may cause us to feel fear even when there is no real threat. For example, if a romantic partner threatened us somehow in the past, any similarities with a new partner could trigger a reaction. Trauma can also be caused by cultural and social factors as well. Growing up in a home or community where we felt unsafe or helpless can spark a lifetime of fearful experiences and behaviors.

Fear of loss is a major trigger and can stem from past experiences or future expectations of losing something or someone important to us. This could be loved ones, possessions, or our sense of personal identity (ego). It arises from our inherent need for security and can manifest as the fear of abandonment, rejection, or failure.

Then there is the fear of the future when we do not know what is going to happen and use our imagination to project negative scenarios. Often, fear of the future can ignite uncertainty about what lies ahead, worry about potential outcomes, or anticipation of negative events or consequences. This is commonly called worry, or anxiety when it is particularly intense or chronic.

Fear, when misused, is extremely self-limiting. It moves from the realm of a protective mechanism to an excessive or irrational place that can hinder personal growth, limit opportunities, and negatively impact your overall well-being.

Some common phrases you may speak to yourself internally when influenced by fear are:

- "I don't feel safe."
- "Something bad is about to happen. I know it."
- "I think they might hurt me."
- "I am worried that I might die."
- "What if something terrible happens?"
- "I can't stop worrying about this."
- "What am I going to do?"
- "I really don't want to face this."

The great irony is that when fear has become pathological and toxic, we actually act *against* our self-interest and tend to manifest the very scenarios of which we are afraid. We literally attract what we fear the most. For example, you may worry that you are not good enough for your current romantic partner and they are destined to leave you. You can't help but imagine scenarios where you are left devastated and have to shamefully tell your friends and family about the failure. This fear leads you to either seek approval in the form of needy behaviors that push them away, or to detach your emotions and act as though you never wanted this person in the first place. You become increasingly distant, or overbearing, or both.

Meanwhile, your partner has no idea why this is happening. They were entirely intent on loving you as you are, but as your behavior changed, so did their feelings. They begin to show more distance and indifference themselves, then conflicts arise and, before you know it, you leave them for a replacement partner in anticipation of being left first. In your mind, this way, you've at least controlled the outcome of the situation. All the while, the relationship would have progressed naturally if you had just moved past that fear of inadequacy and abandonment by self-satisfying your psychological need for security. Instead, you manifested what you feared the most.

# FRUSTRATION

> **Frustration, like a dripping faucet, can slowly erode the foundation of our spirits.**
>
> **— Unknown**

Frustration is a feeling of dissatisfaction, disappointment, or irritation that arises when our efforts to achieve a desired outcome are blocked or met with obstacles. It is a common emotional response that's triggered when we fail to accomplish a goal or fulfill a need we believe we have in that moment. Frustration is usually related to feelings of being stuck, helpless, flawed, or powerless. Instead of going with the flow of life and flexibly adapting, we become fixated on controlling the situation or outcome through manipulation.

The experience of frustration often involves tension or agitation, as we feel thwarted or hindered in our progress. This can quickly lead to anger, particularly when frustration is triggered by external factors, such as challenging circumstances, uncooperative people, or unexpected setbacks. Road rage is a common example. Even the most innocuous setback, delaying your arrival by *seconds,* can send us into fits of rage because we were hindered by something outside of our control. We are also often the source of our own frustration. Internal factors such as high expectations, perfectionism, or lack of confidence can contribute to feelings of frustration.

We may exhibit different responses when confronted with frustration. Some may feel motivated to persist and find alternative solutions, while others may become overwhelmed, angry, or demoralized. We may even choose to displace our frustration onto others in the form of aggression and abuse. If not managed effectively, chronic frustration can have negative effects on mental and physical health, leading to stress, anxiety, or feelings of inadequacy.

You might also hear frustration expressed as:
- Disappointment
- Anguish
- Irritation
- Vexation
- Annoyance
- Aggravation
- Exasperation
- Discouragement
- Impatience
- Letdown
- Agitation
- Indignance
- Overwhelm
- Feeling Pressured
- Feeling Rushed
- Confusion

We feel frustration for a variety of reasons, but it most often stems from unmet expectations, obstacles, or difficulties in achieving our goals. This causes frustration because we have a plan in mind and lack the flexibility to gracefully deviate from that plan. We become sensitive to the fact that we aren't going to get something, or somewhere, in a manner that we believed we need to in order to *feel fulfilled*. We intended to show up at 5 o'clock sharp and arriving at 5:01 means that we are fundamentally flawed, which threatens our psychological need for security. These feelings are often exacerbated when we think about the future often and play scenarios in our head of exactly how we want things to happen.

Another instance where we feel frustrated is when something has happened, or has failed to happen, that we believe is unfair or unjust, such as witnessing unfair treatment, experiencing inequality, or feeling powerless in the face of injustice. That powerlessness is at the heart of frustration.

You can notice when you are frustrated by recognizing some of these statements in your internal dialogue:

- "Why won't this work out the way that I want?"
- "This isn't fair."
- "Things never go my way."
- "All I want is for this to happen. Is that so much to ask?"
- "I wish they would just behave the way that I want them to."
- "How am I supposed to achieve my intention with this obstacle in my way?"
- "Why do they always do this?"
- "I just want to quit and start over."
- "Of course this happened, just my luck."
- "I can't believe they got in my way."
- "Now what do I do?"

Our culture encourages immediate gratification over delayed gratification. When we have to wait, frustration may arise as our patience wears thin, and the feeling of being stuck and not making progress gets stronger. Complex problems or challenges are often difficult to solve or overcome, but our conditioning to seek instant solutions conflicts with reality. Usually, the underlying psychology here is that we are somehow not safe if we are not making progress. There is something coming to get us and we need to stay one step ahead. This psychology underpins a lot of our experiences with work and career ambitions.

Miscommunication, ambiguity, or a lack of clear information can also contribute to frustration and often occurs when expectations are not clearly defined or when there is a breakdown in the exchange of information. Many relationships and work environments are damaged by this process.

We covered the fear of the unknown in the previous section; however, it bears repeating here that anytime we are feeling fearful, we can also become frustrated. Fear, by its very nature, means that something is happening that we can't stop or control. Our need for security convinces us that we should mitigate uncertainty and gather enough information and resources to exactly predict future outcomes. But since we cannot, we become frustrated.

A primary contributor to frustration is the inclination to set such rigid and high standards that virtually no one or nothing can meet them. We often justify that these are standards of excellence or quality

*The 5 Levels of Conscience*

and, sometimes, they are. But most of the time, they are borne out of our desire to ensure that things unfold exactly as we envision. If our standards are not met, we become frustrated because now, our subconscious tells us we are no longer worthy of love and admiration from ourselves or from others. This feels like an existential threat.

This is not to say that we should never be disappointed and never try to influence the outcomes of situations. Rather, we can approach situations with flexibility, positivity, and an element of acceptance. That way, when obstacles arise, we can approach them with a clear head and a healthy frame of mind. In addition, if things don't happen the way we want them to, we have a healthy response and are open to the idea that things may work out even better than we had imagined.

**LEVEL 1 — CONNECTION TO OTHERS**

# GREED

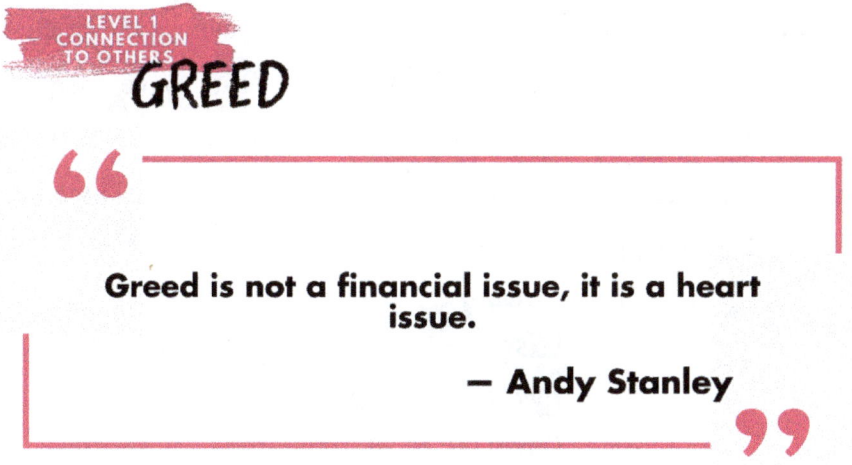

> Greed is not a financial issue, it is a heart issue.
>
> — Andy Stanley

Greed is when your desire for something becomes so overwhelming that you are willing to sacrifice things that matter to you in order to obtain that object of desire. That desire could be for wealth, power, possessions, resources, sex, or anything else we feel will support our need for security. It is usually insatiable and leads us to acquire and accumulate more than what is necessary or reasonable, regardless of the consequences or the impact it will have on others.

Greed can lead us to prioritize our self-interest and personal enrichment above ethics, values, or morals that we all share in common. This is very deeply tied to narcissistic and Machiavellian behavior. Greed is the mother of hoarding, exploitation, manipulation, and dishonesty. It is also a gateway to anger because the underlying desire is already so intense. This is not to say that we are wrong when we desire more for ourselves. Greed is an extreme and unbalanced form of desire, characterized by an excessive and selfish accumulation of resources, driven by an insatiable hunger that cannot be satisfied, even once the desire is fulfilled. Greed can have negative consequences not only on a personal level, but also on a sociological scale, as it can perpetuate inequality, injustice, and unethical practices.

It is also called:
- Craving
- Lust
- Avarice
- Covetousness
- Rapacity

## The 5 Levels of Conscience

- Cupidity
- Acquisitiveness
- Materialism
- Mammonism
- Gluttony
- Selfishness
- Grasping
- Voracity

Greed typically arises from a scarcity mindset based on a belief that there is not enough to go around and that we will somehow be less deserving of love without the fulfillment of a certain desire. The mind incorrectly concludes that competition and hoarding can solve the problem. This scarcity mindset can drive us to accumulate more than we need out of fear of missing out on something, not having enough in the future, needing to rely on others, or out of the fear that we will not be accepted by ourselves or others without obtaining or achieving something. This type of behavior often leads back to frustration when setbacks occur. Think of the body builder who injects themselves with damaging chemicals in order to gain more and more unnecessary muscle.

Greed can be a trauma response stemming from deep-rooted feelings of loss or inadequacy, as well as of the fear that we may need to rely on others one day who may let us down or betray us. This can be particularly worrisome if we tend to take advantage of others and fear their retribution. Some claim to pursue excessive wealth or possessions as a means of feeling secure or protecting themselves from future hardships, but the reality is that there is no way to be completely secure against everything that may happen.

The desire for social status and recognition can also lead to a craving for more wealth or possessions. Our culture often promotes the idea that success is equated with material wealth and, thereby, happiness. This can create a sense of competition and drive us to acquire more in order to gain prestige and maintain the narcissistic image of our mind. It can also lead us to manipulate others into believing things about us that aren't true, like lying about our accomplishments.

If you tend to have a high need for control, power, or admiration, you may be more prone to experiencing and acting upon greed. This can come from a variety of sources, such as upbringing, exposure to media, and societal influences. A simple, everyday example of greed in action could be giving into the impulse to cheat at a board game because your desire for admiration from others overwhelms your ability to relax and enjoy the moment. Greed is arguably the most destructive emotion we have and is responsible for many of the greatest injustices of our time and times past.

You can recognize greed through phrases such as:

- *"I really want that and would do anything to get it."*

- *"I can't stop thinking about it. I have to have it."*

- *"These are all mine!"*

- *"I earned this, and I don't need to share with anyone."*

- "I'll just take it. No one will ever know."
- "What they don't know can't hurt them."
- "If I don't get what I want, there will be consequences."
- "I know I don't need it, but I want it anyway."
- "I know I have what I need, but that isn't enough."
- "I don't have to help them; they should help themselves."
- "That would be better in my possession than in theirs."

It is important to distinguish greed from normal and healthy desires. As destructive as greed can be, it is not optimal for us to completely eradicate desire. Some eastern philosophies assert that "all suffering arises from desire." While this is arguably true, the conclusion that we should eliminate all desires is a fallacy. First of all, this is impossible to do, and second, suffering is a very important part of the human condition. We cannot improve in any aspect of life without a certain amount of suffering and no great human accomplishment has come without suffering. No pain, no gain, as the saying goes. The critical distinction is not to attach our self-worth, our well-being, or our sense of safety to these desires and, thereby, *suffer more than is necessary*.

A very simple way to recognize the difference is to evaluate our reaction to the potential of achieving or not achieving the desire. A desire that has inspired greed will be put on a pedestal in our psyche. We feel like it will somehow change our entire life, our self-image, or our inner being, and not achieving the desire will result in subsequent damage. A healthy desire will not significantly affect any of these aspects of ourselves. Imagine two athletes competing for a gold medal in the Olympics. One fails, achieving silver, and concludes their life's work is worthless and so are they. This leads to catastrophic failure and misery that lasts for years. Another athlete fails, achieving bronze, and concludes that it is an honor to have reached such incredible heights of human achievement. They then share the blessing by creating youth programs that positively impact thousands of lives. The critical difference between the two is a healthy vs unhealthy relationship to the roots of their desires.

##  THE IMPULSE TO CONTROL

> **At the end of the day, you can't control the results; you can only control your effort level and your focus.**
>
> **— Ben Zobrist**

All the emotions of level one will inspire the impulse to control people, outcomes, and situations. This impulse actively seeks to know everything that has been and will be. It seeks to achieve complete certainty and build a reality that supports our needs, wants, and insecurities at any cost. It does not trust anyone or anything, including our Creator, and not even ourselves. It is ruthless and destructive tunnel vision that causes suffering in all that it touches and lends itself to what we know as narcissistic and Machiavellian behavior.

This impulse is particularly destructive to the psyche because we cannot truly have complete control of anything except for our own thoughts and actions. As the proverb goes, "We plan; God laughs." This keeps us chasing a level of security that we can never truly achieve, harming ourselves and others in the process. Imagine someone who spreads rumors and falsifies their achievements in order to get a promotion they are not ready for.

This impulse can also become very dark and pathological when we desire to have complete control over others. We are trying to take away the very thing that makes them a sovereign being, which is their free will and autonomy. In order for our psyche to justify this behavior, we will subconsciously reduce their worth and importance, saying things like, "they deserve this treatment," or "they are not worthy of autonomy." This is called dehumanization. There is a sort of God complex that seeks to remove the free will of others and create a reality suited to our own needs at the expense of anything in the way. This is a likely contributor to the justification of slavery.

Recognizing the impulse to control can be a valuable step toward developing self-awareness and making positive changes in our behavior. When we have difficulty relinquishing control, the evidence of it shows up in our inner dialogue. We might say things like:

- "I know what's best for everyone."
- "It has to be done my way or not at all."
- "I can't trust anyone else to handle this properly."
- "If I delegate this to someone, they may not do it right."
- "If you want something done right, you have to do it yourself."
- "I can't stand when things don't go according to plan."
- "I'm just trying to help by taking charge."
- "I don't like surprises or deviations."
- "I'll take care of everything. Just leave it to me."
- "You're not doing it correctly. Let me show you how it should be done."
- "I want this, and I don't care what it takes to get it"
- "It is not fair that things are happening this way."
- "I really hope this doesn't happen."
- "What will I do if things don't turn out how I want them?"
- "I need things to happen in this manner so I can feel a certain way."
- "If this doesn't happen, there will be negative consequences."
- "I don't feel safe. I need to do something."

*The 5 Levels of Conscience*

Notice how your body feels when you are clinging to control. You might feel tension, tightness, or discomfort. You may experience anxiety, panic attacks, or fits of rage. A sinking feeling in your chest or your stomach may be present. You may feel lightheaded. You should also notice your thoughts. Notice any recurring beliefs that drive the need for control. These are usually tied to the belief that I am not safe, I am not enough, and I need something to happen a certain way in order to be safe and approve of myself and my experience in life. Review the list above because many of the phrases mentioned we might not choose to say out loud. Instead, we hold them inside as thoughts that affect our well-being. However, they are just as potent in our minds, or in our subconscious, as they are when spoken aloud.

The desire for control makes it difficult to find the balance between personal interests and respecting the autonomy of others in order to maintain healthy relationships. When acting upon the impulse to control, the other party becomes an opponent onto which we seek to assert our will. This quickly turns into a battle and, as Eckhart Tolle writes in his bestselling book, *The Power of Now*, "Whatever you fight, you strengthen, and what you resist, persists." We cannot feel safe without a feeling of autonomy, and we will even act against our own interests to exert this need. This is a common cause of people refusing to accept help from others during times of struggle.

There may be scenarios, however, where you need to exert a certain amount of control over those you have responsibility for. Think of your pets or children, for example. In these scenarios, make sure to disengage the pathologic aspects discussed in this section, and approach the task playfully while accepting that you may not succeed initially. This keeps their autonomy in consideration and does not dehumanize them.

## MANIPULATION

> **Manipulation is a contagious disease, much more dangerous than the flu because it can endure for a lifetime.**
>
> **— Dorothy McCoy**

As we live more and more often in level one, giving into the impulse to control, manipulation will begin to arise in our lives. Manipulation refers to the act of influencing or controlling situations and/or others using cunning, deceit, aggression, intimidation, or other indirect means. It involves using tactics or strategies that shape someone else's thoughts, beliefs, or actions in a way that benefits the manipulator, often at the expense of the manipulated. That is what makes manipulation especially sinister; it is typically directed toward other people at their expense.

We engage in manipulation for various reasons, depending on our motivations, circumstances, and personality traits. Ultimately, though, if we are manipulating, we feel unsafe and out of control.

Unfortunately, manipulation can be very addictive because it can inspire a sense of power and self-satisfaction, as well as achieve dominance in relationships, situations, or environments.

Manipulation can also be used as a defense mechanism to protect ourselves from perceived threats or vulnerabilities. We may manipulate others to guard against rejection, criticism, or harm by hiding aspects of ourselves or our past. We often see this behavior in those of us who struggle with low self-esteem. We may give in to level-one behaviors in an attempt to avoid confronting our perceived inadequacies like hiding our affection for someone. We often see manipulation occur when we are afraid of losing someone's love, attention, or support. This could be lying about something we did or charming them with excessive affection and compliments.

Often, when we don't display strong communication skills, we will resort to manipulation to get what we want. It is our way of expressing our needs, wants, or concerns. We may shame others or use passive-aggressive tactics to influence the other person without them realizing what is happening. These are learned behaviors that are reinforced through past experiences and continue to be strengthened over time. If we have observed or experienced successful manipulation as a means of achieving our goals, we may continue to employ such tactics.

Keep in mind that fear, frustration, and greed are all very effective ways that others use to manipulate *us*. Making us feel unsafe or stoking an intense desire for wealth are two very common ways people use to manipulate us into behaviors that benefit them at our expense.

Ultimately, consistent manipulativeness causes a mistrust in *others* as a projection of our inability to trust and respect ourselves and our Creator. This will cause a deep-seated internal dissatisfaction because our innermost core knows that it has done something wrong, and wants to progress to level five, but <u>we've calcified the emotion inside a shell of deceit</u>. I will repeat this concept because it is such a crucial one. Living inside level one, fueled by a desire to control people and situations, we will engage in manipulative behaviors such as lying, cheating, stealing, and deceiving. Our innermost core *knows* that this is wrong and will seek to move up to a higher level of conscience. If we refuse, *deceiving and manipulating ourselves in the process*, these emotions will calcify deep within our psyche, festering and inflicting constant damage as we slip further into narcissism and, eventually, sociopathy.

## SOCIOPATHY

Level one can be extremely dangerous if we learn to live there on a regular basis. The more we give in to these emotions and the impulse to control, the more ingrained they become into our personalities. The worst part is that manipulation can be very effective at getting what we *think* we want. Many people have lied, cheated, and stolen their way to the top, but people like this tend to be the most miserable of all because true fulfillment can't be achieved that way. Despite their achievements, they are stuck chasing the most basic fundamental need for safety instead of higher-level needs.

As these behaviors become ingrained into our psyche, we fall further into sociopathy, psychopathy, and other antisocial personality disorders related to narcissism. Some of the widely accepted symptoms of these disorders are ignoring right and wrong, telling lies to take advantage of others, not being sensitive to or respectful of others, and using charm or wit to manipulate others for personal gain or pleasure. These behaviors are all exacerbated by the emotions of fear, frustration, and greed. Let's consider the following examples.

Picture a time when you felt really scared. Maybe you were afraid of failing at work, arguing with a friend, or experiencing drama in your marriage. We might start thinking, "If I disconnect from others, I won't get hurt." We erect shields that we believe protect us from the pain. However, these also shield us from joy.

Frustration works in a similar way. Think about a time when things didn't go your way, and you felt really frustrated. Sometimes, frustration can build up over time. If we keep facing setbacks or feel like we are not being treated fairly, we might start thinking, "Why should I care about others if I never get what I want?" This bitterness can make us want to "even the score" by taking advantage of people or breaking rules. This is likely going through the mind of a thief.

Greed, too, can lead to sociopathy. Have you ever wanted something so much that you'd do anything to get it? This intense desire can take over our thoughts, leading us to completely dehumanize others and behave in the most disastrous ways. We learn to justify our actions and, if successful, are encouraged to continue the behavior. Imagine a corrupt corporation that abuses their employees and destroys the environment.

These patterns can slowly change the way we see the world. We might start believing that we are better off not connecting with others and that rules don't apply to us. The only thing that matters is achieving, acquiring, and controlling.

This is a dangerous path to go down and leads to the most atrocious behaviors of which we are capable. It is very important for us to recognize that these tendencies arise out of a desire to control, and a resulting self-deception, so that we can prevent ourselves and others from falling into this lifestyle.

The first step to move past level one is to recognize when you are engaging in manipulation. Yes, it can be challenging because it often involves subconscious or very subtle behaviors. However, self-awareness and reflection can help to identify when you are on level one. Here are some signs that may indicate you are engaging in manipulation. Keep in mind that we all exhibit these behaviors regularly. None of us are above level one.

— Hidden Agendas: You may have hidden motives or agendas behind your actions or requests, such as seeking personal gain or manipulating outcomes in your favor. This could look like asking for help with something you know how to do, just because you don't want to do it yourself.

- Deception and Dishonesty: You may find yourself using lies, half-truths, or misleading information to influence others' behaviors. This could be as simple as withholding information from your friends because you want to decide where everyone goes to eat. Or, it could be more severe like giving blatantly false information to your romantic partner because you intend to engage in infidelity.

- Shaming and Emotional Blackmail: You may use guilt, fear, or emotional pressure to make others comply with your wishes or to gain their sympathy. Maybe you want your partner to clean and shame them for relaxing on the weekend. Or maybe you threaten someone in order for them to comply with your desires.

- Lack of Respect for Boundaries: You may disregard or violate others' boundaries, ignore their consent, or exploit their vulnerabilities. If someone has told you not to touch them, and you respond by laughing and touching them again, this is a lack of respect for their boundaries.

- Controlling Behavior: If you exert excessive control over others' actions, choices, or decision-making processes in an attempt to limit their autonomy or independence, you are exhibiting manipulative behavior. You may have told your partner that you don't want them to do a specific thing or wear a specific outfit either directly or indirectly. We almost all have.

- Gaslighting: This is when you find yourself undermining, dismissing, or intentionally influencing other people's perceptions, feelings, or experiences, causing them to doubt their own reality. Many times, gaslighting happens subconsciously, so it is important to respect when someone disagrees with us about something someone else has done or said.

- Lack of Empathy: If you minimize or dismiss others' emotions, needs, or perspectives, and prioritize your own interests without considering the impact on others, you have demonstrated a lack of empathy. It is very common for us to disregard others' emotions when we don't want to admit we did something wrong. This can often lead to gaslighting. For example, imagine your partner tells you that something you did made them upset. If you dismiss their feelings instead of taking accountability, you've engaged in gaslighting as a result of a lack of empathy.

*The 5 Levels of Conscience*

- <u>Rule Breaking</u>: If you break rules designed to keep situations fair and equitable, you are manipulating. This could be as simple as cutting in line or as sinister as tax fraud.

- <u>Charming</u>: If you find yourself trying to influence others to feel certain positive emotions in order to get what you want, you've engaged in charming or flattery. This could be giving someone a gift, a compliment, or doing a favor with the intention of getting something in return later.

# LEVEL 1 PRACTICE: ACCEPTANCE

> **Happiness can exist only in acceptance.**
>
> — George Orwell

Once you have realized that you are under the influence of level-one emotions, take a moment to notice any resistance in your mind. Are you experiencing any tension in your body or the desire to cling to specific outcomes you have decided are ideal? In this moment, practice "mindfulness" by bringing your attention to the present moment without judgment. Focus solely on the breath as you empty your mind, slowly increasing the time between each thought. This state of awareness allows you to pause and choose a more conscious response instead of being led by your emotions.

Consider the impact of your thoughts and actions by reflecting on how controlling behaviors make you and others feel. Are your relationships strained? Are you feeling overwhelmed or burnt out?

## The 5 Levels of Conscience

Recognize the negative consequences of the impulse to control in order to help motivate you to seek healthier ways of relating to and engaging with others. This is an ongoing process that requires patience and self-reflection. But if you can develop awareness and understanding of your tendencies to seek control, you can gradually work toward letting them go. This will foster healthier, more balanced relationships and experiences.

In the face of fear, frustration, and greed, we practice acceptance or surrender. Some people do not like the word "surrender". It connotes weakness, which many find repulsive. This perspective is tied to a feeling of inadequacy and insecurity which will cause you to continue to cling harder to a desire for control. In this case, it is the desire to control other people's opinion of you in the form of always appearing strong. While it is my hope that you can move past this misconception, if you cannot, then replace the word "surrender" with "acceptance". Only in a state of calm acceptance can you operate from a position of power anyway. Ultimately, acceptance is the willingness to be guided by our Creator, as opposed to the opinion that our Creator cannot be trusted. I think we can all agree that Creation is a much more powerful force than any of us are, whether alone or in groups.

### Example:

Imagine you are flying on a plane. Everything appears normal. However, you're afraid because you don't fully understand the vehicle and have no control over it. You're feeling exceptionally fearful in the early moments of the flight, particularly while the plane is taking off and making loud noises you don't understand. You breathe more rapidly as you begin to sweat and feel your chest and stomach begin to sink. You become frustrated that you are having to take this trip in the first place, and that the conditions are so uncomfortable. The plane experiences turbulence as you are now almost certain you will crash. You begin to plot your escape and offer to make a deal with our Creator if you are spared. "I promise, I will change if I just make it there alive!" you say to yourself. You then take a deep breath as you realize you've just caught yourself in level one. Now you begin your exercise of acceptance. As you experience complete acceptance of the situation, and even accept the idea of death, your impulse to control begins to subside. You've lived a beautiful life full of love, joy, and meaningful relationships. You had the opportunity to experience life as a human being with all the tools and technology our species has created. Even flying on this airplane in the first place is a miracle! You could die happily in this moment. You breathe deep, relaxing breaths as your sweat dissipates. Finally, you feel deep trust as you allow our Creator to take control and you fall gently asleep.

*The 5 Levels of Conscience*

Here is a simple exercise to move past level one:
1. Assume a position of relaxation, either sitting, lying, or standing, (ideally in child's pose) and face your palms downward in complete release of any metaphorical weapons, tools, tensions, or grasping.
2. Close your eyes and breathe however your body wants to breathe for a few moments.
    a. During these breaths, attempt to empty your mind and let go of any rumination.
- If you are encountering resistance, bring yourself back to your senses by noting things that you can hear, feel, or smell in this moment.
- You can also use the phrase "I wonder what my next thought will be." You'll find this helps to create space.
3. Once you find a bit of space, focus entirely on your breath as you take deep breaths in, and consciously relax every inch of your body and mind as you exhale. Try to relax slightly deeper with each breath you take.
4. As you are exhaling into relaxation, you will speak to yourself, either aloud or silently in your mind, saying:

- "I surrender to the universe in this moment."
- "I lovingly accept what existence has in store for me."
- "Our Creator is on my side."
- "Our Creator knows what's best."
- "I am safe."
- "I am protected."
- "I am at peace."
- "I do not need to be in control of this situation."
- "Everything that happens to me is positive, even if I don't understand why."

Choose any one or more of these mantras. You can even use your own, or none of them, if you feel confident in your ability to achieve acceptance without a mantra. The important thing is to *feel* a sense of surrender and acceptance, which can be accomplished any way you prefer. With each breath, focus on relaxing deeper and deeper as you relinquish control to a higher power that is on your side. Remember that our Creator knows best. What's best for others is also what's best for you, even if you can't understand at the time. We are also limited in our perception, and a seemingly misfortunate delay could have actually saved you from a deadly car accident. Even in death, our Creator could be preventing you from unimaginable suffering worse than death. Also, keep in mind that we are surrendering control of the outcome, not our efforts or our power. You are always most powerful in a state of calm acceptance, completely surrendered to reality.

This exercise works because it first stops the bleeding by ending the circular internal dialogue, or rumination, that keeps us trapped in level one. Then, relaxation allows new dialogue to enter our minds and to be integrated. The dialogue of acceptance works because in that state of universal trust, relaxation, and openness, we have fulfilled our psychology need for security ourselves. We no longer feel the need to control anything. This opens our body, mind, and spirit toward higher levels of conscience.

Moving past level one requires us to *let go*. We detach ourselves from specific outcomes and how we believe things should play out as we surrender to the flow of life. When we practice acceptance, we acknowledge that there are forces beyond our control. We understand that our resistance and struggle do not positively affect anything about the situation and only lead to further suffering for ourselves and for others. No amount of worry is going to keep that plane in the air. No amount of frustration is going to get us a promotion. No amount of greed, lust, or riches will make us love ourselves. Acceptance allows us to tap into a deeper sense of trust in Creation, knowing that there is a greater wisdom at play. In acceptance, we open ourselves to new possibilities, growth, and, best of all, serenity. Through acceptance, we can free ourselves of the terror of the unknown and lack of control. The burden of trying to control everything gives way to the discovery of a sense of peace. In this state, we can accept the idea that even though things have not unfolded as we hoped, they have brought a new opportunity for things to unfold even better than we had imagined. You may lose the relationship you have and find a better one waiting for you around the corner.

Yes, we surrender by giving up something (usually control and desire). But we can also surrender *to* something. For example, we learn to surrender to the lessons and challenges that life presents us with. Doing so allows us to learn and grow as we become open to receiving the teachings they offer instead of feelings of frustration. This will often include accepting the consequences of our actions. This idea can bring up a lot of fear which can be very challenging, especially when we have done things that are considered highly immoral. The important thing to remember is that there is no freedom without acceptance in this situation. You will be forever running from the consequences of these actions, sending you deeper into level one and possibly into sociopathy. It is impossible to live an abundant and joyful life from this space. So, in a way, there is no consequence more detrimental than ensuring a life full of fear, manipulation, and mistrust of everyone around you. We also tend to sensationalize the possible consequences and underestimate the infinite capacity for forgiveness and acceptance in the eyes of others and from our Creator. No matter the consequences, it is always better to accept them than it is to spend a lifetime fearfully avoiding them. That is true courage.

In acceptance we begin to cultivate humility, which opens us to a greater capacity for self-discovery and transformation. We diminish the significance and impact of the consequences of what we fear. Even death is not something to be feared just because we don't understand what awaits beyond. By conceptualizing and accepting the consequences of what we fear, their power over us dissipates.

Acceptance also eliminates frustration by removing our resistance to what bothers us in the first place. This provides us the space to take practical steps toward changing the situation, removing ourselves from the situation, or going along with the situation, but without any negative emotions. We let go of frustration as we realize it serves no tangible benefit.

Finally, acceptance dismantles greed by allowing us to remove our attention from the bottomless pit that cannot be filled. We are no longer concerned with the thoughts and emotions that tell us to accumulate. We are free to focus our attention elsewhere. We are able to accept any outcome life has in store for us without the objects of our desire. We trust that we are capable of dealing with any situation as it comes.

Acceptance requires us to bring our awareness to the present moment and relax in the face of circumstances that we initially believe are not good for us. That means pulling our awareness away from the future and broadening our perspective to include all of Creation, not just us. Usually, when we are not surrendered, we are resisting the knowledge, trust, or peace that is available to us. This is a lot like a drowning person who fights against the lifeguard who is trying to save them. Many lifeguards have gotten bruises, cuts, and broken noses from the victims they were attempting to save because the person struggled to surrender.

When you are experiencing the emotions of fear, frustration, or greed, don't resist them. What you resist persists. Instead, relax and move through them. You cannot eliminate toxic emotions by suppressing them. However, you *can* recognize, acknowledge, release, and replace them.

When you practice acceptance, there are several things you can expect. While everyone's experience may differ, there are some common aspects that often arise. First, you are likely to feel a wave of peace. There is great tension in fear, frustration, and greed that will release almost instantaneously. Acceptance frees you from the obligation of constantly needing to manage every aspect of your life — or worse, wishing you could control someone else's.

When you use these practices, you will undoubtedly take on a more open-minded perspective, as opposed to the tunnel-vision desire to impose your will. Your thoughts and opinions about the particular subject that brought you into level one will begin to shift, allowing you to move past the issue in a more productive manner. For example, your fear of public speaking turns into an appreciation for the chance to practice the skill.

You may find that these practices grow into acts of self-compassion and self-acceptance as you relieve yourself from the role of superhero or master of the universe. You begin to embrace your humanity, including the vulnerabilities and imperfections that go along with it, and embrace the will of our Creator as always in alignment with your well-being. This is a very relaxing and comforting feeling.

You may find that you have reduced stress and anxiety as you allow yourself to set down the burden that comes with carrying the weight of the world on your shoulders. Acceptance allows you to find a sense of ease and flow amidst life's challenges. This is particularly helpful for chronic worriers and those who tend to obsess over worst-case scenarios.

Alignment with authenticity is another major benefit that comes from acceptance. You no longer have to play games with others and can align yourself with your true values. By letting go of external expectations and the need to control others' opinions of you, you can live in a relaxed alignment with your authentic self. As a result, you may see that your relationships with others improve drastically. Why? People feel at peace in your presence because, just as you accept yourself, you accept them and, in turn, invite them to accept themselves. You will encourage others to be human in ways you could not when you were motivated by fear, frustration, and greed. Sometimes, this can be threatening to those who are not ready to accept themselves, and they may lash out at you. Remember, that is part of their journey. Accept that as their issue and do not make it yours by reacting.

The power of acceptance is also evident in our relationships and personal growth. We no longer fear our partner — fear that they will leave us, fear that they will hurt us, fear that they are taking advantage of us. Instead, we relax into the vulnerability that removes our masks and our facades. Vulnerability engenders deeper intimacy and authenticity in our relationships and paves the way for stronger connections with the ones we love.

You will undoubtedly encounter internal resistance. Your mind might say things like, "No! I can't relax. This is dangerous!" or "How am I supposed to accept that I am being treated unfairly?" or "Those people don't deserve what they have if they are dumb enough to fall for my tricks." or "If I accept this situation, I will never be able to change it." Allow yourself to observe these thoughts and emotions without judgment and let them pass. Then, use the exercise of acceptance to help you let go. Recognize that your attachment to a specific outcome or holding onto expectations inevitably leads to disappointment and frustration. They might even move you into anger and sociopathy if this process becomes pathological.

*The 5 Levels of Conscience*

Trust the process. Trust that there is a greater intelligence at work that is supporting you. Believe that challenges and setbacks are opportunities for learning and may work out better than you had imagined. Identify areas in your life where you tend to exert excessive control. Reflect on the impact this has on your well-being and relationships. Then, use the exercise earlier in this chapter to practice releasing that desire for control. You will find that the results are immediate and profound.

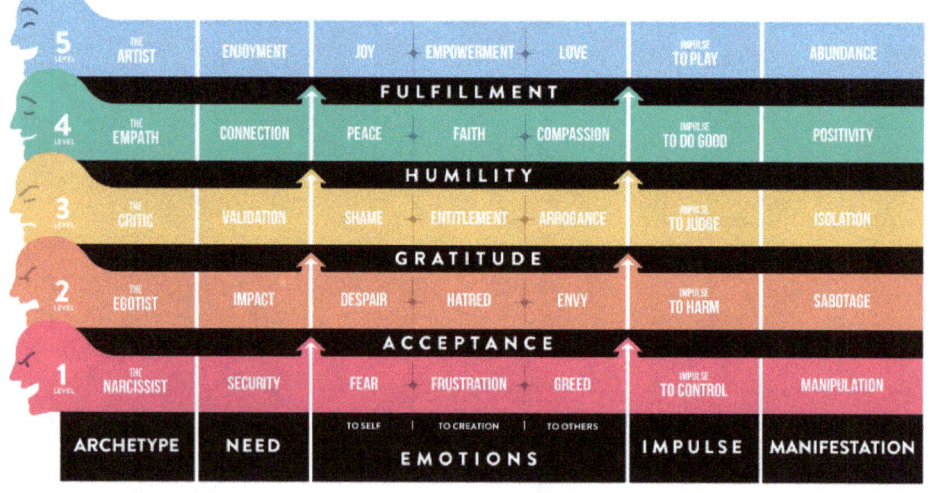

# THE EGOIST

Corrie ten Boom was born in the Netherlands in 1892 to an ambitious Christian family who ran a watch shop. During World War II, the family helped shelter Jews from persecution until they were inevitably arrested by the Gestapo and sent to prison to endure harsh and overcrowded conditions. Her father died shortly thereafter, and all she had left was her sister Betsie as they witnessed unspeakable horrors and struggled to survive.

Despite the circumstances, the sisters did their best to hold steadfast to their faith, sharing smuggled pieces of scripture and inspiring other prisoners. That faith was tested as the rancid straw that served as beds for hundreds of women began to rot nauseatingly and attract fleas that would bite them incessantly.

One night, as they sat together wondering if they were to survive these conditions, Betsie recalled a passage they had read earlier that morning. "Rejoice always, pray constantly, give thanks in all circumstances;" (1 Thessalonians 5:14-18). They reluctantly gave thanks for everything they could note, from being assigned a room together to the fleas that bit them at all hours of the day.

As their health weakened, they were permitted to remain in the barracks and knit socks for work as they traveled the barracks to spread scripture to the others. They quickly realized something. The guards began to refuse to enter their room and harass them. Why? Because of the fleas. The very fleas that challenged their spirit to persevere became the very reason they were able to avoid further torment.

Betsie succumbed to the harsh conditions, but despite this tragedy, Corrie never gave up until the day she was released in 1945. From then on, she dedicated her life to spreading the message of gratitude that saved her life, inspiring others for nearly four more decades. Corrie's story reminds us that, not only does gratitude improve our spirits, but that many times circumstances that seem misfortunate at first, end up being blessings.

## LEVEL 2 ARCHETYPE
# THE EGOIST

> **Egotism is the anesthetic which nature gives us to deaden the pain of being a fool.**
>
> — Dr. Herbert Schofield

## The 5 Levels of Conscience

The archetype for level two is the egotist. Our ego is our sense of individuality and separateness from others, and the egotist lives entirely in this world without ever feeling in union with others or with our Creator. The egotist and narcissist are very similar but with a few key differences. While the narcissist acts in their own self-interest because they do not recognize the autonomy or interest of others, the egotist acts in their own interest because they believe it is the right thing to do and that you should do the same. The narcissist cares more for admiration and power to build up the image they project to others, whereas the egotist's primary concern is material gain and a personal feeling of superiority. The narcissist's main weapon is manipulation and control, while the egotist's is force and willpower. Where a narcissist may intentionally manipulate someone and blame their victim saying, "If they allow me to manipulate them, then they deserve it," the egotist may steal from someone who is vulnerable and justify it by saying, "If I don't steal from them, someone else will." The egotist can be highly successful and sometimes may even be highly ethical. The problems occur when the egotist does not get what they want and cannot exert their power. This is when the level two emotions of despair, hatred, and envy will arise. Once again, keep in mind we are all both narcissists and egotists at times, and there is need to judge ourselves or others for being human.

On level two there is a sense of acceptance, but that acceptance could be that you are bad and others are better than you, or that your situation will never improve, or that others are wrong and evil. You realize you can no longer control the person or situation, which leads to an impulse to do the next best thing, which is to harm them or to harm yourself in protest. This obviously manifests as the sabotage or damage of self or others. During this response, the subconscious is seeking to gain a sense of importance and impact as opposed to the sense of security and control from level one.

Let's look at the underlying psychology as well as each emotion in-depth and review how to recognize them, as well as what it takes to move past them. As a reminder, it is important to see these emotions and behaviors as fluid. We are not stuck on any one emotional level. We are not any one archetype. We are all always moving up and down the chart. The point is to identify the emotions, the behaviors they cause, the way those behaviors manifest so we can work to move away from toxic patterns as we reach for healthier ones.

### LEVEL 2 NEED
# IMPACT

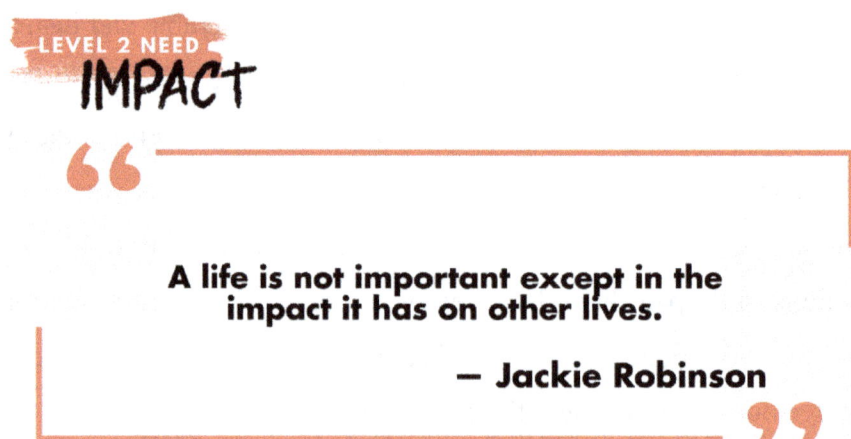

> **A life is not important except in the impact it has on other lives.**
>
> — **Jackie Robinson**

## *The 5 Levels of Conscience*

Our impact refers to the effect we have on the people and the world around us, as well as on ourselves. It is the mark we leave, the difference we make, and the influence we have through our actions, skills, and overall presence. Impact is what makes us relevant or important. This could be through small moments on a daily basis at work or in our community, or through historic events that are talked about for ages. Once we feel secure and safe, our next desire is to make our mark on the world. This instinct is as old as the cave paintings our ancestors left for us to discover thousands of years later. The level-two emotions are all coping mechanisms for dealing with a compromised sense of impact.

Ideally, the impact we have would be 100% positive on everyone and everything around us. Unfortunately, we live in a world with competing interests that is not ideal, and any impact is better than no impact at all to our subconscious. The only thing worse than infamy is irrelevance. Irrelevance means no one cares about us which, as beings who are completely interdependent, could pose an existential threat. When we are under the influence of a level-two conscience, our ego has been compromised, our sense of personal power is threatened, and our instincts tell us to do the quickest and easiest thing, which is to cause harm or damage. If we can cause harm or damage, we have proven that we are impactful and, therefore, relevant. In these moments, we don't even care about the consequences because we are already gravely threatened. We may even welcome harm as a way to feel something different at all, or in the form of a death wish.

We don't have to be rendered completely impotent for these feelings to be triggered. It could be as simple as seeing someone that we don't like in control of something we care about. Or if we see someone who possesses something that we want, making us believe that we will never be able to accomplish that feat or obtain that object. It can also happen when we lose in a competition to someone. These types of events make us feel some amount less influential and powerful. This can trigger our envy, hatred, or despair as a result.

Having impact and influence gives us a sense of competence, ability, and possibly even power. Our ego loves this. Effecting change on the world gives us a release of endorphins, which tells us that we matter and that our experience is relevant. This will create a positive feedback loop that encourages us to continue the behaviors and effect more change in the world, even if it is negative. We may then justify it in our minds as positive so we have a continued excuse to enjoy the high. This can lead to great wealth and destruction at the expense of others and, many times, even self-destruction.

It is important to have a healthy relationship with this dynamic so that we can recognize when we are the ones being impacted and influenced by it. We can check ourselves by asking:

- "Am I doing this because it makes sense or because I am sad, hateful, or envious?"

## The 5 Levels of Conscience

- "Will this behavior cause harm to myself or others in the short or the long run?"

- "Am I trying to prove anything to myself or others right now?"

- "Can I tap into what I am grateful for in this moment, or will I encounter resistance?"

Keep in mind that it is arguably impossible for our actions to be purely beneficial to all. There is always some perspective from which we can view an action as good or evil. Sometimes, we are even confronted with a decision between the lesser of two evils. The ultimate check is within our emotions. Can we truly say that we are devoid of level-two emotions and can easily tap into our gratitude as we perform this action? In gratitude, we don't need to have any more influence, impact, or power than we do already. We are free to behave from a place of fulfillment and can clearly see our version of a positive impact on the world.

## DESPAIR

**Despair is a narcotic. It lulls the mind into indifference.**

**— Charlie Chaplin**

Despair is an intense and overwhelming feeling of hopelessness, sadness, or utter discouragement. It is a state of mind where you may feel a profound sense of loss or emptiness. You believe that you can no longer impact the situation and there is no possibility of improvement or positive change. Despair often arises from a combination of challenging life circumstances, personal setbacks, or a prolonged sense of dissatisfaction or disillusionment. You have accepted a state where nothing will ever improve. This is a common response when we do not get what we want, or our expectations of ourselves and our lives fall short. This also tends to push us toward envy and hatred when we see others meeting the expectations we fall short of. These emotions all tie back to how our ego believes the world should be in order to satisfy our psychological need to feel relevant and impactful. This is in contrast to the existential self-preservation that is the motivator of level one.

When experiencing despair, we may begin to lose our appetite, our desire to connect with others, and our will to overcome obstacles and achieve our goals. Apathy is very common, and we will tend to be a burden to those around us. We will generally start to attack ourselves consciously or subconsciously. This may look like negative self-talk, or subconscious self-sabotage.

## The 5 Levels of Conscience

You might hear despair referred to as:

- Hopelessness
- Desolation
- Anguish
- Distress
- Desperation
- Misery
- Melancholy
- Gloom
- Sorrow
- Dejection
- Depression
- Sadness
- Helplessness
- Defeat
- Victimization
- Powerlessness
- Fragility
- Apathy
- Boredom
- Loneliness
- Grief

We typically feel despair when we have accepted a circumstance as both negative and unchangeable. This leads to a loss of hope and a sense of powerlessness that causes us to question our worth, purpose, and the meaning of life itself. We can all remember times when we felt our backs were "against the wall" and we did not have any good options. The lack of a plan and feelings of incompetence can lead us into despair.

However, despair can also be influenced by our individual temperament, life experiences, and coping mechanisms. Some of us may be more prone to experiencing despair due to inherent sensitivity or past traumas. Maybe we were severely heartbroken and chose to default to despair and hopelessness instead of trying to find another lover.

Despair can have various causes, such as the loss of a loved one, the breakdown of relationships, chronic health issues, financial struggles, or the feeling of being stuck in a life that lacks fulfillment. It can also arise from external factors, such as societal injustices, political unrest, or witnessing widespread suffering. You may find yourself and others talking about the state of the world and feel that things are getting decidedly worse. Without the ability to impact the situation, this can lead to a sense of helplessness, discouragement, and despair.

A person who has lost a job faces financial struggles and feels hopeless about finding new employment might face despair. Or it could be a student who has repeatedly failed exams and feels like they will never succeed academically. A survivor of a natural disaster who has lost their home and belongings will likely feel a deep sense of despair. A person who has been betrayed by a close friend or partner might experience immense heartbreak and despair.

While despair is often thrust upon us by outside forces, it can also be the result of our poor decisions and the consequences we have to face as a result. That is particularly difficult because we tend to

## The 5 Levels of Conscience

blame ourselves and fall into patterns of negative self-talk and decreased self-esteem.

You can recognize despair when you or others use phrases like:

- "I don't see a way out of this."
- "I feel completely lost and hopeless."
- "I can't bear this pain anymore."
- "It feels like nothing will ever get better."
- "I'm overwhelmed and don't know what to do."
- "I feel like giving up."
- "There's no point in trying anymore."
- "I'm trapped and don't see any options."
- "I can't imagine a future that is better."
- "I feel like I'm drowning and can't catch my breath."

As despair becomes chronic, it can turn into what is commonly known as *depression*. Just like all emotions in the framework, the more often we live inside a particular emotion, the more engrained that emotion becomes in our psyche. This makes it increasingly difficult to break out of the pattern. Take comfort in knowing that, although difficult, it is possible to recover as countless people have in the past.

The first step is to dis-identify with the word and to *believe* that you can recover. This involves shifting your perspective from "I *am* depressed" to "I am *currently suffering from* depression." The former is a rigid state with no room for improvement, while the latter is a temporary state that *will* improve. Once you have disidentified, you can use the tools in this book and others to recognize your depressive patterns and take steps toward recovery. It will not be easy, but each moment and each day you make progress will build momentum to keep you away from despair as a reflex. Remember to also consult with your medical provider if you believe you are suffering from depression.

## HATRED

**Hatred, which could destroy so much, never failed to destroy the man who hated, and this was an immutable law.**

**— James Baldwin**

Hatred is a strong feeling of disdain, scorn, or disrespect toward someone or something. It is a negative emotion that arises when we view others as inferior, unworthy, undeserving of respect, evil, or destructive in some manner. There is a dehumanizing element toward the other party. Contempt is a form of hatred that involves a sense of superiority, where one feels a significant gap between themselves and the object of their contempt. Spite is another common form that arises when one has been harmed by another and wishes to harm them in return.

Hatred can be directed toward individuals, groups, institutions, or even ideas. It may stem from a perception of moral or intellectual superiority, personal biases, or a deep-seated resentment toward a particular person or group and their behaviors or states of being.

In hatred, we tend to wish the worst for others, which can ultimately lead us to take things into our own hands in the form of aggression. The desire for revenge is a common manifestation of hatred when we have been harmed by someone else. It will cause tunnel vision and obsessive thoughts, as well as feelings of tension and rigidity. In this reactionary state, the cycle of harm will not stop until one or all parties are destroyed.

Hatred can manifest through mocking, attacking, belittling, or dismissing others, and it often involves a lack of empathy or understanding of the person and the situation. For these reasons, this emotion can be harmful to relationships and social dynamics, as it creates a barrier between individuals and inhibits open communication and mutual respect. It can lead to strained interactions, conflicts, and a breakdown of trust with those who do not feel the same hatred toward those same individuals or groups. This is a common pattern seen in politics and even sports fanatics.

Hatred also includes:

- Disdain
- Disrespect
- Scorn
- Derision
- Disregard
- Disparagement
- Disapproval
- Disgust
- Sneering
- Contempt
- Spitefulness
- Vengefulness
- Bitterness
- Resentment

Hatred arises within us for various reasons. The primary cause is rooted in our perceptions, beliefs, and judgments. We may feel hatred toward others when we perceive them as inferior, ignorant, unjust, unethical, or unworthy of respect. Disdain can also result from deep-seated prejudices, biases, or past negative experiences that shape our perception of certain individuals or groups. The revenge response occurs as a way for us to re-establish ourselves as equal or superior when our ego says we have been harmed or diminished.

But make no mistake, hatred can show up in small ways as well as big ones. When we feel hatred, it often stems from a perceived threat to our own egoic identity or values. It can be triggered by behaviors, opinions, or actions that challenge or

## The 5 Levels of Conscience

contradict our own beliefs or norms. It can also be a defense mechanism, protecting our ego from vulnerability or discomfort by distancing ourselves from others. For example, we might have contempt for something a person says or does, even if we don't have any problem with them otherwise. Maybe you wish to be a great singer, and in hearing a friend's great voice, you suddenly feel a wave of contempt for them because it sparked the insecurity you feel about your current skill level. Now, you either no longer wish to be around them until you can re-establish your self-image, or you verbally berate them either aggressively or subtly.

Hatred can be identified when you hear things like:

- "I can't believe how stupid they are."
- "They don't deserve any respect or consideration."
- "I can't stand being around them."
- "They're beneath me."
- "They'll never amount to anything."
- "I have no patience for their ignorance."

- "They're a lost cause."
- "I can't even pretend to listen to their nonsense."
- "They're not worth my time or attention."
- "I can't comprehend how anyone could be so clueless."
- "I can't believe they would do that."
- "Their behavior is unjustifiable."
- "They are completely bad and deserve the worst."
- "I hope terrible things happen to them."

Often, we show hatred for large organizations or ideologies. For example, a political party, a corporation we deem as unethical, or a non-profit that supports a cause we don't agree with. While we might never say we hate a particular person, we might say we hate the organization they belong to. This emotion of hatred is still just as toxic a force on the self, whether directed at a particular person, an ideology, or the world itself. The negative emotion comes from within and impacts our psyche like a poison we drink in the hopes that the object of our hatred will suffer. In addition, organizations, companies, countries, and other large groups are ultimately made up of people. As we show hatred for the intangible organization, that emotion is ultimately directed at the people who support and constitute the organization.

In that way, hatred can be detrimental to relationships and hinder our ability to empathize and connect with others. It can perpetuate stereotypes, prejudice, and discrimination, creating division and fostering a toxic environment. Most often, it is the very characteristics our egos reject in our current or past selves that inspire us to hate others. So, in a way, hatred for others often includes an element of self-rejection because all of us experience all ranges of emotions and behaviors to certain extents.

## LEVEL 2 — CONNECTION TO OTHERS
# ENVY

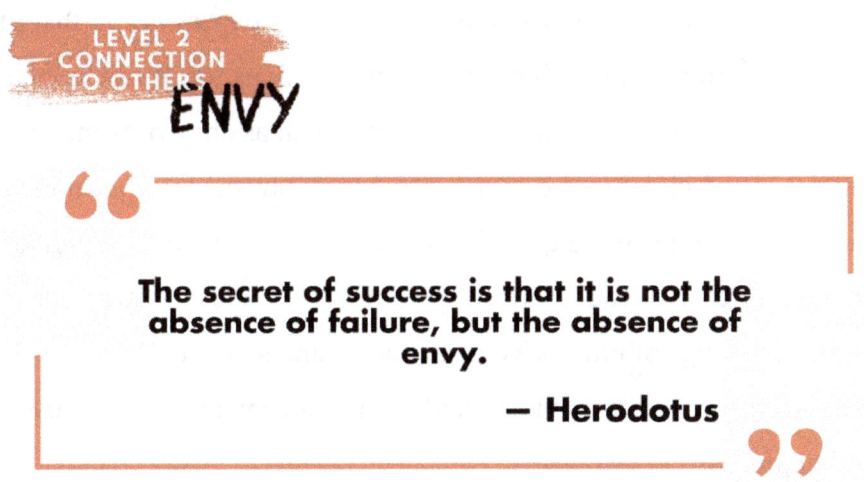

> "The secret of success is that it is not the absence of failure, but the absence of envy."
>
> — Herodotus

Envy is a complex emotion that arises when we desire something possessed by someone else, which then causes us to feel a sense of discontent or resentment because we lack it ourselves. It is usually associated with money, but it could be inspired by many other things, such as looks, popularity, influence, or recognition. Envy involves a mix of longing, admiration, and a feeling of injustice that arises from a perceived inequity that we cannot immediately change or impact. There is very often a sense of envy beneath many expressions of hatred as well. Instead of admitting we envy someone, we may choose to hate them instead to avoid the vulnerability that comes with admitting someone has something you desire.

Envy can take two forms, one more concerning than the other. A person can want the same thing another person has and allow that emotion to grow out of control (e.g., *I wish I had a nice car like that*). On the other hand, a person can want the *exact* thing another person has (e.g., *I want* that *car*).

Envy often occurs when we compare our experience to that of others, focusing on the achievements, possessions, or attributes that we covet. It can manifest in various forms, such as envy of someone's material possessions, career success, physical appearance, relationships, or personal qualities. However, this type of comparison can just as easily lead us to despair. Envy is a destructive force, inspiring feelings of bitterness, inadequacy, and self-pity. It can strain relationships, breed resentment, and hinder our own personal growth and happiness.

It is often expressed by the following:

- Jealousy
- Covetousness
- Resentment
- Grudge

## The 5 Levels of Conscience

- Desire
- Longing
- Bitterness
- Spite

Our sense of fairness can be a catalyst for envy as well. We might feel others have what we don't, but should, have. Maybe you feel someone was "fed with a silver spoon" and that you should have more than them because you worked much harder than they did. One of the primary reasons we struggle with envy is our psychological need for recognition and a feeling of personal power or impact. We often compare ourselves to others to measure our worth and success, leading to feelings of inadequacy when we perceive others as having more or achieving more. Our culture doesn't help as it glorifies material possessions, appearance, and accomplishments, which can further fuel our envy.

People who struggle with envy might say:

- "I wish I had their looks. They're so effortlessly attractive."

- "They always get the best opportunities handed to them. It's not fair."

- "Why do they have so many friends? I wish people liked me that much."

- "I can't believe they have such a luxurious lifestyle. I wish I could afford that."

- "They are so talented and successful. I wish I had their skills."

- "It must be nice to have such a loving and supportive family."

- "They are always traveling to exotic destinations. I wish I could do that."

- "I'm so envious of their popularity and social media following."

- "Why is everything always so easy for them? I wish I had their luck."

- "I can't stand how happy they always seem. It's like they have everything, and I have nothing."

Most people tend to equate physical possessions with success, and success with happiness and fulfillment. When combined with a "scarcity mindset," these two opinions lead to a very toxic form of envy. A scarcity mindset is the idea that resources are highly limited, and it is difficult to achieve goals. This leads us to conclude that when someone else gains or achieves something, there is now less available for us to gain and achieve. This perspective will have us rooting for, and enjoying, when others fail, even our own family members, and possibly even sabotaging them ourselves. When we take this perspective and we see someone else succeed, we feel like something is being taken from us. A common analogy for this attitude is "crabs in a bucket." This refers to the way crabs will intentionally pull down other crabs at the top of the bucket, preventing them from escaping for no apparent productive reason.

Envy is catastrophic to healthy relationships and detrimental to our self-image. Whether it is friends, family, or colleagues, any amount of envy will become a barrier to genuine connection and will manifest as an inability to feel happiness for others, as well as subconscious attempts to sabotage them. There will always be a subconscious tension that both people can feel, and neither is comfortable with. When experiencing envy, we focus only on what we are lacking, which stifles our ability to be satisfied or fulfilled. This is a very uncomfortable feeling that leads to rumination and an inability to feel good about ourselves and our life situations.

## LEVEL 2 IMPULSE
# THE IMPULSE TO HARM

> Make a habit of two things: to help; or, at least, to do no harm.
>
> — Hippocrates

The impulse that arises from level two is one that leads us to harm, minimize, or eradicate others so that we do not have to deal with the insecurities we feel internally. Something has triggered our ego to feel diminished or impotent, and our subconscious wishes to feel powerful and impactful again.

Many times, we want the object or the person to no longer exist in our space, or to do enough damage to them in order to gain a feeling of superiority that improves our compromised self-image. We see this commonly when someone challenges an opinion that we hold. We tend to personally identify with our opinions and take a perceived attack on those opinions as an attack on our ego. This causes us to lash out at the person making the argument rather than the argument itself. Although, sometimes, we may later take it out on innocent people, animals, or objects around us. Other times, we take it out on ourselves either mentally, emotionally, or physically.

Hatred and envy are very strongly connected to anger. However, even despair can foster anger as well. When we feel trapped, our survival instinct kicks into high gear. We feel as if the whole world is against us and no one is rooting for us. We victimize ourselves into helplessness and, in a state where we have nothing to lose, we lash out at others without restraint. You can recognize the impulse to harm by your internal dialogue. It may sound like:

- "I will make them pay."

- "They deserve this."

## The 5 Levels of Conscience

- "They've wrong me in the past and I need to get back at them."

- "They are a threat and must be eliminated."

- "They think they are better than me. I'll put them in their place."

- "There is not enough room for both of us at the top."

- "I can't stand them; someone needs to shut them up."

- "They aren't worthy of mercy or forgiveness."

- "They had it coming anyways."

- "I'm worthless and don't deserve to be happy."

- "I am terrible and should be punished."

As we lash out and do harm to others, we are also harming ourselves. We are all interconnected, and anything we think, feel, or do to others, we also do to ourselves. It is common for us to feel guilt and shame after acting upon these impulses. Shameful as it may be, after we satisfy this impulse to harm and feel powerful again, we open space for relaxation and gratitude for the success of our aggression. Although, similar to the desire to control, once the other person is harmed, you will inspire resistance and opposition from the other party and their associates. This will result in a constant struggle and a downward spiral that leads to mutual destruction. As Ghandi says,

"An eye for an eye will leave the whole world blind." It is also possible, though, for the satisfaction of this impulse to lead to greed, and an addiction to the power felt by exerting dominance on others. You may even see someone influenced by this greed attempt to exert control over others after harming them by forcing them to perform certain humiliating acts and speech. They've been brought down to level one.

Possibly the most tragic way level-two emotions manifest themselves is in the impulse to harm oneself. This can lead to minor harms like unconscious accidents, thinking of or saying hurtful things about ourselves, or punishing ourselves with dangerous behaviors such as drinking, smoking, drugs, or overeating. However, in the most extreme cases, level-two emotions can lead to physically harming ourselves, as well as suicidal ideations and behaviors. When these thoughts become frequent and repetitive, it is a lot more likely that they will lead to actions. If you or anyone you know are experiencing these thoughts on a regular basis, please seek professional help immediately.

## *The 5 Levels of Conscience*

## SABOTAGE

> *Leaders who are kind of insecure or egocentric, they basically sabotage themselves.*
>
> — **John C. Maxwell**

When we give in to our impulse to harm, we begin to sabotage ourselves or others. This can be in very loud and explicit ways, but also very quiet and subtle ways. Let's look at self-sabotage first.

Self-sabotage refers to those conscious or unconscious actions, behaviors, or thought patterns that hinder our well-being and cause physical or emotional harm. We often sabotage ourselves when feelings of inadequacy arise. We feel worthless, and our subconscious works to ensure that our life aligns with how we feel about ourselves. This may cause us to lose confidence and believe that failure is our destiny. Then we may engage in self-defeating behaviors to avoid taking risks or pursuing goals. We only allow ourselves to feel the amount of happiness we believe we deserve, and our subconscious will do its best to keep us where our self-esteem says we should be.

Self-sabotage is also a result of low self-esteem and self-worth due to deep-seated negative beliefs about ourselves. These beliefs can stem from past experiences, criticism, or internalized societal expectations. Perhaps we tried very hard to win a contest or to get a job, but we failed. Perhaps others told us we would fail and then criticized us after we did. These events are internalized as negative beliefs about ourselves and take the form of self-criticism, avoidance, and intentionally creating obstacles for ourselves. These actions serve as a self-fulfilling prophecy that confirms the belief that we are unworthy or incapable of achieving any future goals we may have.

Despair tends to cause negative self-talk, self-doubt, and self-limiting beliefs that can contribute to self-sabotage. When we believe that we are not capable, deserving, or worthy of success, we usually undermine our efforts and sabotage our own happiness and fulfillment.

The list of self-sabotaging behaviors is long, with some of them explained below:

- **Procrastination** prevents us from achieving our goals in a timely manner, or even at all, if it turns into countless unfinished projects. Many times, this is due to a resistance to come to terms with the gap between the outcome we perceive in our conscious mind, and the outcome our subconscious believes will actually occur. We have almost all experienced procrastination at work or school.
- **Self-criticism** causes psychological harm and prevents us from performing our best. We believe that criticizing ourselves will motivate us to perform better. However, that is almost never the case. Telling ourselves we aren't good

enough is more likely to cause us to underperform and, sometimes, to not even try. We may even criticize ourselves when things are going well because we believe we don't deserve what we want, and that whatever positivity that comes in our lives.

- **Negative self-comparison** can cause us to focus on our perceived flaws. This keeps us from expressing our gifts, and very often leads to self-criticism. We may have something interesting to contribute to a discussion but stifle ourselves because we aren't confident in our competence.

- **Drug or alcohol abuse** is a way for us to escape reality. It causes real and immediate damage, yet we continue to do it because the impulses become too strong and overwhelm us.

- **Impulsive and dangerous behavior** can many times arise from a subconscious desire to harm ourselves. Some people call this having a "death wish." Examples of this include driving dangerously and taking unnecessary risks that provide no potential benefit.

- **Overeating** is similar to drug and alcohol abuse in that it provides a temporary respite from the feelings we refuse to process. While the damage done is not as immediate as drugs, the problem compounds over time, making it arduous to unwind.

- **Physical self-harm** is often a cry for help and an attempted catalyst for change. However, sometimes, it is the result of a genuine self-hatred and a feeling that we deserve punishment. It could even be an attempt to alleviate our suffering permanently in the form of suicide.

On the other hand, when your desire to harm is focused on others, you will attempt to sabotage them. This can be mild or severe and can come in the form of:

- **Undermining** someone's projects, tasks, or goals to make them look incompetent or ineffective. This could look like calling someone out in a team meeting unnecessarily.
- **Spreading rumors or gossip** is a common way to tarnish someone's reputation, opportunities, or credibility. Even if the rumors are true, we are ultimately giving in to our impulse to harm.
- **Withholding information** is something people do to ensure that important information or resources others need are not available to them. This could be a team member you are in competition with and with whom you will not share useful resources..
- **Taking credit for others' work** is a common sabotage tactic. We might claim credit for someone else's achievements or ideas, denying them rightful recognition.
- **Excluding or isolating** is an emotionally damaging ploy where we leave someone out of social circles or important discussions to make them feel ostracized or ignored. This

## The 5 Levels of Conscience

is commonly achieved by making fun of or insulting others to establish a frame that they would lower your status.

- **Passive-aggressive behavior** is something we all fall victim to. It is marked by showing hostility, sarcasm, or offering backhanded compliments to undermine the other person's confidence. Maybe you call attention to someone's fashion choices by complimenting them, even if you feel otherwise.
- **Micromanagement** is a sabotage technique people use when they have power over others. Excessively controlling or interfering with someone's work or personal life prevents them from making independent decisions and flourishing in their unique manner.
- **Setting unrealistic expectations** is often described as setting people up to fail by assigning unattainable goals or tasks to make them look incompetent.

Physical or emotional harm is the most extreme form of sabotage we can exhibit under the influence of level-two emotions. This can manifest as verbal abuse, physical attacks, attempts at homicide, or all of the above. This is the type of behavior we most often think of when we think about our desires to harm others and what we most commonly imagine when under the influence of level two. However, because the repercussions of acting on these thoughts and impulses tend to be severe, you will more often see someone settle for the behaviors listed above.

Ultimately, whether your attacks are directed consciously or subconsciously at others or at yourself, there will always be an element of self-rejection and self-destruction involved in this manifestation. We are only separate from others in our minds. All it takes to realize this is to look at the Earth from the perspective of space. The entire planet could be thought of as one living organism, of which we are one tiny part. If we truly embodied that perspective, would we ever truly want to harm it or to harm others instead of helping them?

We only feel the need to do harm to something that threatens our ego and its sense of power, relevance, and impact. That threat could be our own characteristics or characteristics in others that trigger us. Most often, these are actually the characteristics that we hate about ourselves. We may lash out at our partner for relaxing on a Sunday because we feel the need to prove that we are not lazy. The more we tend to attack others and attack ourselves, the more credence we give to these imagined threats and the further we move away from resolving the insecurities that fuel them in the first place. This ultimately leads to the sabotage of all aspects of your life, from your friendships to your finances and even your health, safety, and well-being.

## LEVEL 2 PRACTICE: GRATITUDE

> *Gratitude is not only the greatest of virtues, but the parent of all the others.*
>
> — Cicero

Gratitude is a powerful force that involves acknowledging and appreciating the goodness, blessings, and positive aspects of our lives, both significant and trivial. When we cultivate gratitude, we shift our perspective and open ourselves up to a myriad of benefits that can enhance our well-being and transform our lives. It is a simple yet profound practice that can work wonders in our lives. It has also been shown to improve physical and mental health, enhance relationships, boost resilience, and foster overall happiness and fulfillment.

Gratitude is not just a fleeting feeling. It is a practice that can be cultivated and integrated into our daily lives which keeps us higher on the chart more consistently. We can all benefit from this practice in all aspects of our lives on a daily basis. This means finding gratitude not only in moments of joy and abundance, but also during times of difficulty and struggle. It is through these challenging moments that gratitude becomes even more transformative, as it helps us find meaning, resilience, and growth in the face of adversity. In this way, gratitude becomes a gift to ourselves and others.

Keep in mind you can also practice gratitude for things you do not have yet. This is a common method used in manifestation practices.

## Example:

Imagine you have lost a job and submitted more than one hundred resumes for consideration. You received very few replies, and the ones that resulted in interviews were not followed by an offer. This has led you to despair and a sense of worthlessness. Now, you are likely giving off negative energy in every phone call and interview about a new job. You begin to feel hatred toward the arduous application process and the companies who refuse to consider you—not to mention the economy and leadership of your country. Your attention turns toward your friends with good jobs. "Why can't I have what they have? I hate my industry." Envy settles in and leads right back to despair and worthlessness in a continuous cycle. Finally, you realize you are in the cycle, and by just taking the time to stop and connect with gratitude, you shift your energy from negative to positive. You feel grateful for the experience you have, and the good health to be able to work a job in the first place. You feel you are highly capable, and employers would be lucky to have you. This new perspective leads you to see opportunities in roles and industries that you might not have tried before. When you have interviews, you demonstrate resilience and impact them more positively than you did when influenced by despair. It is hard to turn down a potential employee who exudes positivity and gratitude. It is only a matter of time before you are aligned to the role that is perfect for you in that moment.

**LEVEL 2 EXERCISE**

The following is a simple practice to use when you recognize you are operating on level two:

1. Assume a position of relaxation, either sitting, lying, or standing, (ideally in child's pose) and face your palms up to the sky as if to accept a gift from our Creator.
2. Close your eyes and breathe however your body wants to breathe for a few moments.
   - During these breaths, attempt to empty your mind and let go of any rumination.
   - If you are encountering resistance, bring yourself back to your senses by noting things that you can hear, feel, or smell in this moment.
   - You can also use the phrase "I wonder what my next thought will be." You'll find this helps to create space.

3. Once you find a bit of space, focus entirely on your breath as you take deep breaths in and consciously relax every inch of your body and mind as you exhale. Try to relax slightly deeper with each breath you take.
4. As you exhale into relaxation, reflect on the things you are grateful for, starting with the simple joys and gradually expanding to encompass larger aspects of your life. Slowly speak them aloud or to yourself, one by one. As you do this, let the feelings of gratitude fill your being. Visualize the positive aspects of your life and let the gratitude wash over you. Spend a few minutes in this state of gratitude before slowly coming back to the present moment. Here are some examples of things you might say:

- Thank you, Creator, for the blessing of _____
    a. Running water
    b. A warm house
    c. Friends and family
- I am so thankful for _____
- Every day is a gift and a blessing.

Fill in the blanks with anything you can think of that you are genuinely grateful for. Your resistance might say, "I have nothing to be grateful for!" This is very common, and everyone has felt this way under the intense influence of level-two emotions. The reality is, though, that there is *always* something to be grateful for. It could simply be the fact that you have running water in a climate-controlled home, unlike the vast majority of every being that has ever existed on Earth. It could be the immense riches you've accumulated, or the modest paycheck you received this month. It could be for exceptional height and good looks or the fact that you have all of your limbs functional and intact. The important thing, once again, is to *feel* the emotion of gratitude. So, use whatever you can think of that you feel genuine gratitude toward.

This is the primary exercise you can perform in moments where you've recognized level-two emotions or behaviors. The following are some more that you can practice on a daily basis to lower potential resistance and to keep yourself at higher levels of conscience on a more consistent basis.

— Exercise 1: Gratitude Journal

You have certainly heard this advice before. Perhaps you scoffed, doubting that it would work, or maybe you thought it was a great idea, but you haven't tried it yet.

— Exercise 2: Gratitude Letter

Let me encourage you to buy a gratitude journal and commit to writing in it daily as you reflect on what you are grateful for. Be specific and detailed in your descriptions. Take your time. If you don't like to write extensively, use keywords or draw pictures. This is for your eyes only.

Choose someone in your life for whom you are grateful, whether it's a family member, friend, mentor, or even a stranger who has made a positive impact. Take the time to write a heartfelt letter expressing your gratitude and appreciation for them. Be specific about the ways they have enriched your life. You can choose to deliver the letter in person, send it by mail, or even read it aloud to them in video form and send them the file. You could also choose not to send it at all and keep it for yourself. This exercise not only cultivates gratitude but also strengthens your relationships.

### Exercise 3: Gratitude Walk

Go for a walk in nature, preferably in a peaceful and serene environment. As you walk, focus your attention on the beauty and wonders around you. Notice the colors, sounds, scents, and textures of the natural world. With each step, express gratitude for the elements of nature that bring you joy and peace. This exercise allows you to connect with the present moment, deepen your appreciation for the world, and cultivate a sense of gratitude for the abundance of nature.

Gratitude practices are effective primarily because the feeling of gratitude cannot coexist with feelings of despair, hatred, or envy. Have you heard of anyone grateful for their misery? Or someone who expresses appreciation for the opportunity to envy someone? When we regularly engage in gratitude practices, we cultivate a growing sense of awareness and mindfulness of the positive things around us, and the negativity dissipates like darkness exposed to the light. By focusing on the positive aspects of our lives and acknowledging the goodness in the world, we feel comfortable with the amount of impact and influence we've had in life.

In despair, we are victims, lacking energy and belief. Gratitude serves to help us realize that, while we may suffer misfortunes, as long as we are breathing, there are positive aspects of our lives, and our circumstances can always be improved. As we focus on these positive aspects, we find the strength and resolve to move forward in an effort to multiply them.

In hatred, we focus on the negative aspects of others, of circumstances, of experiences, or of phenomena. We feel that these somehow threaten our self-image or the amount of relevance and power we have. In gratitude, we focus on the positive aspects of our lives, of life in general, and even of the very things that were once the focus of our hatred. This causes us to relax and realize that we are not threatened so we can focus on the positive will that we can exert instead of the negative.

In envy, what we have is not enough, and what others have is the solution to all our problems. In gratitude, we are completely content with what we have and don't have any problems that need solving in the first place. There is no need to even think about what others have at all.

Overall, gratitude shifts our focus from what is lacking in our lives to what we already have. It helps us develop a positive perspective and appreciate the present moment. When we cultivate gratitude, we become more aware of the blessings and opportunities that exist in our lives, even when faced with adversity. This change in perspective allows us to experience a sense of abundance and fulfillment, leading to a greater sense of well-being. In this state, there is no need to harm anyone or anything, only to grow the blessings that we already have. In fact, harming someone else would open the door to retaliation and threaten our safety, which would be crazy.

When you practice gratitude, you foster a sense of support from individuals and our Creator. No matter what happens or what circumstances you are dealing with, you remain optimistic. This works out the muscles of patience and keeps your mood at an elevated state for longer periods of time.

This process will increase your resiliency and prevent you from falling into toxic behaviors and emotions. You will have more energy and belief in problem-solving and will not fall into self-victimization as often. This will lead to more consistently healthy decisions, behaviors, and activities that result in positive life outcomes. For example, a bad day at the golf course will inspire you to hit the range more often instead of lashing out at yourself and others.

In the same manner that acceptance opens your mind to a new perspective about the situation that triggered your emotions, gratitude will do the same. For example, the envy of your friend's success now turns into inspiration, or someone's optimism that once triggered annoyance now becomes a goal for you to embody.

Many will also argue that, in a state of gratitude, you will begin to attract more of the things you want and desire as a result of the laws of attraction. Just as we find in the world what we have in our minds most often, we would notice more blessings as we are more consistently aware of them. In this case, we are certainly more likely to give to others who will then reward our generosity with sincere appreciation. It is also illogical to think that we would attract more blessings if we went through life ungrateful and thankless in our interactions. An important distinction worth noting is that many proponents of this law of attraction suggest that when you desire something specific, the best practice is to feel gratitude for already possessing your object of desire. Accordingly, your subconscious can't fully distinguish between feelings, thoughts, and reality, which will cause your reality to align with the thoughts and feelings of gratitude for your object of desire.

You also strengthen interpersonal bonds and condition yourself toward empathy by leveraging gratitude. You will feel more love, support, and satisfaction in your relationships, which will cause the other person to enjoy your presence more. You will both feel more valued, and it will serve as a positive feedback loop that will increase the resiliency of the relationship.

Overall, the power of gratitude lies in its ability to reframe our perspective, nurture emotional well-being, and create a ripple effect of positivity that enhances our lives and might help others in our social circle.

*The 5 Levels of Conscience*

# The 5 Levels of CONSCIENCE

| ARCHETYPE | NEED | EMOTIONS (TO SELF / TO CREATION / TO OTHERS) | | | IMPULSE | MANIFESTATION |
|---|---|---|---|---|---|---|
| 5 LEVEL — THE ARTIST | ENJOYMENT | JOY | EMPOWERMENT | LOVE | IMPULSE TO PLAY | ABUNDANCE |
| **FULFILLMENT** | | | | | | |
| 4 LEVEL — THE EMPATH | CONNECTION | PEACE | FAITH | COMPASSION | IMPULSE TO DO GOOD | POSITIVITY |
| **HUMILITY** | | | | | | |
| 3 LEVEL — THE CRITIC | VALIDATION | SHAME | ENTITLEMENT | ARROGANCE | IMPULSE TO JUDGE | ISOLATION |
| **GRATITUDE** | | | | | | |
| 2 LEVEL — THE EGOTIST | IMPACT | DESPAIR | HATRED | ENVY | IMPULSE TO HARM | SABOTAGE |
| **ACCEPTANCE** | | | | | | |
| 1 LEVEL — THE NARCISSIST | SECURITY | FEAR | FRUSTRATION | GREED | IMPULSE TO CONTROL | MANIPULATION |

*The 5 Levels of Conscience*

# THE CRITIC

Circa 304 BCE, Ashoka was born to then Emperor Bindusara as one of many sons who were potential heir to the throne of Magadha on the Indian subcontinent. His father disliked his rough skin, instilling doubt and shame from an early age. When it came time to determine the next emperor, Ashoka didn't even want to participate, although his mother finally convinced him to do so.

In hopes of gaining the approval of his father, Ashoka participated in a brutal war of succession, killing several of his brothers as he emerged victorious and became the third emperor of the Mauryan Dynasty. This experience instilled a deep propensity for brutality as he conquered several regions through war and violence. As he conquered the Kalinga region eight years later, he decided one morning to take a look at the aftermath of a fierce battle. There, he witnessed firsthand over 100,000 men and animals brutally killed and taken captive. The battlefield was littered with corpses, the putrid smell of decay, and the helpless cries of the wounded.

Ashoka recalled the cries of his slain brothers and the toll it took on his mother. How different were these men from him, really? Each one had a mother just as his own. Was this the legacy he wanted to leave for his subjects? Overcome with remorse in that moment, he renounced violence, asked for forgiveness, and embraced Buddhism for the remainder of his reign.

Ashoka promoted peace, became a zealous advocate for ethical conduct, and played a pivotal role in spreading Buddhism across Asia. He ushered in a period of social reforms focused on improving the lives of his subjects as he built roads, wells, and hospitals for both humans and animals.

Ashoka's reign marked a significant shift on the Indian subcontinent from war and conquest to peace and social harmony. There are over 500,000,000 people who currently practice the doctrines of Buddhism with some of Ashoka's monument still standing over two millennia later. His story demonstrates the transformational power of forgiveness, humility, and atonement.

# THE CRITIC

> "The critic is a man who prefers the indolence of opinion to the trials of action."
>
> — John Mason Brown

## The 5 Levels of Conscience

The archetype for level three is the critic. To the critic, nothing is good enough, and everything must be sorted, categorized, and classified. They take everything too seriously, particularly criticism, ironically enough, and rarely fully enjoy anything. They are highly defensive and tend to complain excessively, and all of this constant negativity can be very off-putting to others. The critic sees everything through the lens of judgment, including themselves, which is fueled by feelings of shame, entitlement, and arrogance. A critical nature can highly discourage taking positive action out of shame, fear of being judged, or feeling as though one deserves results without action. This can lead to a very lonely and stagnant experience. We all have an internal critic that will rear its head from time to time. Our task is to learn to recognize it and reflect on its message objectively instead of allowing it to generate toxic emotions and behaviors.

On level three, we have a calm acceptance of life as it is and may even experience gratitude for the blessings therein, but in excessive gratitude or excessive expectations, we can believe we are inferior or superior to others a result of our judging mind. We do this because of our psychological need to feel validated or admired and comparison can serve to quickly support or refute whatever level of validation we seek.

Level three is unique in that the emotions associated with it are all generally destructive over time, but they also have elements that can lead to positive outcomes. Shame can be a catalyst for fundamental growth and change in behaviors. Arrogance can keep you away from pitiful behaviors, as well as reinforce a positive self-image and an entitlement to greatness that inspires incredible work and accomplishment. Level three is like a fork in the road that represents a great opportunity to settle into positive levels of conscience but can also be one of the hardest to move past because of our collective reluctance to humble ourselves and to forgive ourselves and others.

## VALIDATION

> You'll always feel lonely if you always need validation. People don't like to be around those kinds of people.
>
> — Sherry Turkle

Social validation or approval refers to the general need for us to be accepted, liked, valued, and admired by others. It gives us assurance that our life choices, our abilities, and other aspects of ourselves are seen as generally positive by those around us. This usually includes our thoughts, feelings, and opinions. It also heavily involves our impact, how we feel about that impact, and how we believe others perceive that impact.

Our innate need for validation is crucial in keeping our species functioning together and in an orderly manner. It's the social contract we've created to hold each other accountable and prevent us from falling into hedonistic chaos. Imagine a world where no one cares what any other person thinks about their behavior. It would be nearly impossible to accomplish any coordinated effort. We need a certain level of social harmony and validation to thrive in an interconnected world. However, the desire for validation can easily become pathological. We can relinquish our autonomy and personal truth in the name of conformity. This becomes a prime opportunity for a narcissist to control our behavior for their own benefit by shaming us. We will stifle ourselves and refuse to share our gifts with the world for fear of being judged and losing the validation we so deeply crave. It can also cause us to chase after material possessions that we believe others admire even if we don't care about them.

External shaming is one method that can trigger our desire for validation, but we can just as easily trigger it ourselves in our minds. We may see someone receiving praise and feel that we now need similar praise. Maybe we see an advertisement for something that we want but can't afford and now feel inferior to those who have it. Maybe we did something or said something that we now regret and are embarrassed by, so we need someone or something to validate our behavior. The common theme here is that there is something external that we believe will satisfy this desire for validation.

Many times, the level of validation we seek is benchmarked by the expectations we have of ourselves. When that benchmark is misguided or too high, this can cause us to chase a level of validation that we can't achieve. This keeps us stuck in level three unless we learn to break the cycle. Having high expectations of yourself is good, but we tend to believe we should punish ourselves if these expectations aren't met in the hopes that the negative reinforcement will inspire us to achieve more. This is rarely the case and more often will cause procrastination. If you choose to keep very high standards for yourself, it is crucial to internalize humility and self-forgiveness so you can detach yourself from outcomes to avoid falling into this pattern.

Because validation is such an important part of our human condition and crucial to our success, we have to learn how to handle it prudently. When reflecting on our behaviors and desires, we can ask ourselves:

- *"Am I behaving this way naturally or because I am feeling shame, entitlement, or arrogance?"*
- *"Am I judging myself or others right now?"*
- *"Am I seeking the approval of anyone but myself?"*
- *"Can I completely validate myself internally or do I need others to know and approve of this to feel happy?"*

Provided that we are not currently in a moment of intense shaming by a large group in consensus, our desires for validation are almost always misguided. We have the ability to provide ourselves with all the validation that we need at any moment. We can do that using the level three practice of humility that you will learn shortly, but it's also wise to assess the expectations we set for ourselves to see if they are reasonable and beneficial. Otherwise, we can end up back in level three more often than necessary.

# SHAME

> **Shame is like a wound that is never exposed and therefore never heals.**
>
> — Andreas Eschbach

Shame can be one of the more profoundly and deeply unsettling emotions. It is an internal prison that holds us captive because it is something we tend to shroud in secrecy. The things that bring us shame are the things we want to hide from the world. However, just like in nature, the things we hide from the light cannot grow. Shame is a result of us concluding that we are undeserving of validation and support. It buries us in darkness through a feeling of unworthiness, many times as a result of our perfectionism.

At its core, shame is the belief that we are inherently flawed, unworthy, or fundamentally deficient. Our internal critic tells us these things, and we accept them as true. We then feel that we have done something wrong or are in a situation that casts us in a negative light. The secrecy and silence that follow grow stronger as they feed off our natural tendency toward self-judgment and inner criticism. This can turn into compulsory negative self-talk that stifles our growth and destroys our self-image.

You may hear shame described in other ways. But make no mistake, the terms below all carry the same meaning as shame and have the same impact on our well-being:

- Embarrassment
- Humiliation
- Guilt
- Regret
- Disgrace
- Mortification
- Chagrin
- Self-reproach
- Reproach
- Indignity
- Ignominy
- Abashment
- Inadequacy
- Inferiority

Shame is often triggered internally from our own feelings of failure or not measuring up. But, as we dig deeper, we can almost always find some external standard, norm, or expectation at the root of shame. It could be societal expectations, cultural norms, or values learned in our upbringing that leave us with a distorted sense of self. Maybe our parents were great athletes, but we prefer intellectual pursuits.

Shame can come in the form of guilt regarding specific actions that we deem to be wrong, or it can blanket our psyche, affecting our self-esteem, relationships, and overall well-being. In this state, we can feel shame even when we know we have done nothing wrong. Victims of abuse often struggle with shame long after the traumatic event has happened, and with no logical trigger or response.

Often, it is our early experiences, such as neglect, abuse, or critical parenting, that compel us to believe our critic when it tells us we are unworthy. The more often we experienced these things, the more difficult it will be to unlearn the pattern. Think of the overbearing parent that will not accept their child unless they become a doctor.

Specific events or failures that challenge our self-image can also trigger shame, reinforcing the belief that we are inadequate. But it doesn't require any trigger at all. Feelings of shame can arise at the most random and inopportune times. When they do, they can be paralyzing, preventing us from living authentically and opening up to the world. We want to hide our imperfections, flaws, and vulnerability because we don't want to be rejected, ostracized, or judged.

Ironically, shame can also come in the form of judging yourself to have too much relative to others. There is even a condition labeled "Sudden Wealth Syndrome" which is characterized by isolation and guilt after coming into wealth quickly. The common theme among all feelings within the realm of shame is our internal critic creating a subjective expectation that conflicts with our external reality. These expectations are what we believe to be the requirements for us to feel validation, support, and admiration.

Shame causes intense desires to isolate. But the isolation only deepens the shame, eroding our self-esteem and locking us away in this awful feeling of imprisonment.

Shame reveals itself in the following types of self-talk:

- "I'm so embarrassed."
- "I feel so humiliated about myself."
- "I can't believe I did that. I'm such a loser."
- "I don't deserve anything good."
- "I should have known better."
- "I'm so disappointed in myself."
- "I can't face anyone after what happened."
- "I'm such a screw-up."
- "I wish I could disappear."
- "I'm so ashamed of who I am."
- "If they find out about this, they will think less of me"
- "I can't let anyone know."

Shame is destructive both internally and externally as it bleeds into our work, family, and relationships. It throws up barriers between us and others, and between us and opportunity. We erect walls to shield ourselves from being seen and exposed. This makes it difficult to forge deep, meaningful connections. Shame can also distort our view of others' intentions. We may feel as if we're under the microscope or in danger of being found out. That can lead us to mistrust others or, at least, push them away. We deprive ourselves of the very human need to be connected, loved, accepted, and understood.

Wearing shame is like wearing shackles. Everything becomes harder as it assaults our courage and self-compassion. Though there are supportive people around us who want to help us, shame builds prison walls that are thick and high.

## LEVEL 3 CONNECTION TO CREATION
# ENTITLEMENT

> **Entitlement is simply the belief that you deserve something. Which is great. The hard part is, you'd better make sure you deserve it.**
> — Mindy Kaling

Entitlement is a complex and multifaceted emotion. It is based on the idea that a person deserves special treatment, certain privileges, or other advantages on the basis of something other than merit. Our ego says that we require certain treatment and if we don't receive it, that means we aren't what we think we are. This is highly invalidating.

Entitlement is generally evidenced by an extreme lack of patience and a demanding demeanor.

Entitlement arises when our internal critic says that we are inherently deserving of something. The critic tells us that, because of who we are, who we know, or some other factor unrelated to merit, that we should receive certain benefits, recognition, or privilege. Then, we believe it! We believe our physical or personal attributes, social status, or other perceived superior qualities place us above others. This causes us to feel like certain rules and norms that apply to others don't apply to us at all, which leads us to behave in ways that others will see as disrespectful. We may believe that we can skip the line at a bar because we spent so much money there the previous week. We may believe that there must be something wrong with anyone crazy enough to turn us down on a date. We may even shame and chastise a close friend who doesn't go excessively out of their way the moment we demand something from them.

Entitlement is fueled by a sense of self-importance, unrealistic expectations, or an overinflated sense of self-worth relative to others. Keep in mind that a healthy sense of self-worth and confidence are all important. These are not the same as entitlement, however, because entitlement is an emotion that disregards the rights, needs, and worth of others. Entitlement is generally sparked in comparison to others, while healthy confidence and self-worth are internal and not dependent on others.

## The 5 Levels of Conscience

You may hear entitlement also described as:
- Privilege
- Presumption
- Supremacy
- Self-importance
- Unearned advantage
- Condescension
- Self-entitlement
- Superiority
- Elitism
- Pretentiousness

We often attribute entitlement to the most beautiful, wealthy, famous, or politically connected among us. But that would be a mistake, since almost anyone can fall victim to the effects of entitlement. Entitlement can transcend material wealth or physical appearance, as it stems from an internal belief that you deserve special treatment or privileges. It can manifest in people from all walks of life, regardless of their external circumstances. Here are few examples:

**Workplace entitlement:** An example is an employee who feels that he or she is entitled to promotions, raises, or special privileges without putting in the work to get there. This person might assume that, because they have worked for the company for a certain length of time, or are related or connected to someone in authority at the company, they should receive special privileges without the necessary effort, competence, or contribution.

- **Relationship entitlement:** A partner who expects their needs to be prioritized at all times without reciprocating or considering the desires and boundaries of their significant other is being entitled. They might feel that their partner should feel lucky to be with them and, therefore, should do whatever it takes to make them happy.

- **Social entitlement:** Someone who believes they are entitled to skip lines, receive preferential treatment, or demand immediate attention in public settings, disregarding the needs and rights of others is displaying social entitlement. These people can get loud and rude when something in public doesn't go their way.

- **Parental entitlement:** Parents who expect others to accommodate their children's needs and desires without teaching them empathy, responsibility, or respect for others are being entitled. These people often assume that their child is special and should not be subjected to the same rules as other children.

- **Academic entitlement:** Students who believe they deserve high grades or special treatment simply for attending class, without putting in the required effort, studying, or meeting academic expectations are displaying academic entitlement. We have seen plenty of scandals involving celebrities who pay their children's way through school because their children don't feel they should have to put in the same effort as others.

**Financial entitlement:** Individuals who feel entitled to financial assistance or resources without taking personal responsibility for their financial well-being or making efforts to improve their financial situation are an example. This is often the case in situations where people work the system to get as much as they can, even when they don't truly qualify for funds or resources meant for those in real difficulty.

**Customer entitlement**: Customers who believe they are entitled to unreasonable demands, discounts, or preferential treatment from businesses without considering the challenges faced by the service providers or the policies in place are behaving in an entitled manner. We have all seen videos capturing this behavior, as employees are at the mercy of angry and demanding customers.

**Beauty entitlement:** Individuals who feel entitled to special treatment or privileges based on their physical appearance, assuming they are more deserving or superior to others solely due to their looks are great examples of beauty entitlement.

- **Racial Entitlement:** The basis of racism relies on the belief that one ethnicity, color, or origin is inherently superior to another. Some may use their race as a basis for their belief that they deserve something without having to earn it.

Entitlement can emerge from various sources including upbringing, societal influences, and personal experiences. Individuals who were consistently praised or excessively indulged during their formative years may develop an entitled mindset, expecting constant validation and preferential treatment as soon as they ask for it. Cultural factors that promote a focus on individualism or emphasize material success can also contribute to the development of entitlement. This has far-reaching consequences for individuals, relationships, and society.

Entitlement impacts the other party just as it does the person who feels entitled. For example, entitlement can place a burden on relationships because, by its very nature, it brings with it a lack of empathy and consideration for others' needs. It may lead to entitlement-driven behaviors such as demanding special treatment, dismissing others' perspectives, or exploiting relationships for personal gain.

## The 5 Levels of Conscience

Have you ever heard yourself or others say:

- "I deserve special treatment because of who I am."
- "Why should I have to follow the rules? They don't apply to me."
- "I shouldn't have to work as hard as others to achieve success."
- "It's about time people recognize how extraordinary I am."
- "I expect everyone to cater to my needs and preferences."
- "I shouldn't have to wait in line like everyone else."
- "I deserve the best because I'm entitled to it."
- "I shouldn't have to apologize. It's their fault, not mine."
- "Why should I listen to their opinions? Mine are always right."
- "I deserve all the credit for this. It was my idea and effort that made it happen."

Entitlement can limit personal growth and development by fostering a sense of complacency. When individuals believe that they are entitled to success or rewards without putting in the necessary effort or taking responsibility for their actions, they may push people away and miss out on valuable opportunities for growth and learning. They are less likely to push themselves to strive and achieve because they assume the things that they want should be given to them.

Again, it's important here to remember that we are not defining ourselves or others by these emotions. We should not refer to ourselves as entitled, even if we sometimes experience that emotion. That said, consistently succumbing to this emotion can cause conflict and create long-lasting resentment when others perceive the entitled behavior as self-centered or unfairly privileged. This can create tension and strained dynamics within social or professional settings, leading to a breakdown in communication and cooperation. People may choose to avoid someone who behaves in an entitled way because of how it makes them feel. So, remember, we all have an internal critic who will tell us at times that we are owed something. Let this be your trigger to recognize that you are operating on level three.

## LEVEL 3 – CONNECTION TO OTHERS: ARROGANCE

> **Arrogance needs to be explained; confidence speaks for itself.**
>
> — Vitor Belfort

On the flip side of shame is arrogance. Shame and arrogance are both rooted in the emotional judgment of self in relation to others, just with opposite conclusions. In shame, we conclude that we are inferior, and in arrogance, we conclude that we are superior. This emotion is marked by an inflated sense of self-importance, superiority, or the actions of belittling or dismissing others. Arrogance shows itself across all demographics. Regardless of location, economic status, or personal appearance, we can all be influenced by it.

Many times, arrogance is triggered when our inner critic sets its sights on others and, using an arbitrary set of standards and expectations, tells us that others are inferior in some way. This emotion can cause us to underestimate others while overestimating our own abilities, knowledge, or worth. Often, we do this because of an underlying insecurity that we are avoiding. Perhaps we are secretly jealous of someone else's career, so our critic tells us that our height makes us superior to them.

As is the case with many emotions, arrogance can stem from various sources, such as upbringing, societal influences, or personal insecurities. Cultural factors that value individual achievement and competition can be positive. But, when pushed to the outer limits, hierarchical structures can be built that contribute to the development of arrogant attitudes as well. This can be exacerbated if we become used to special treatment. For example, if we excelled at a childhood sport.

When the emotion of arrogance arises, people tend to display an off-putting air of superiority as well as a disregard for differing perspectives. This will lead to an unwillingness to consider alternative viewpoints. We often refer to arrogance in other terms, such as:

- Hubris
- Conceit
- Haughtiness
- Pompousness
- Overconfidence
- Presumptuousness
- Superiority Complex
- Snobbery
- Smugness
- Condescension

Arrogance is not just an offensive stance. Often, this emotion rises as a defense mechanism to mask feelings of inadequacy or to project a false sense of confidence. It becomes a protective measure where our best qualities are put forward aggressively to hide the areas where we are weaker. We may boast to someone about our career achievements to hide the fact we are insecure that we don't have a family.

Arrogance is generally rooted in a deep-seated need for validation or a fear of vulnerability. However, it is also very often rooted in repressed and avoided feelings of shame. It bears repeating that it is not our aim to characterize ourselves or others as arrogant by nature.

## The 5 Levels of Conscience

Arrogance can have a detrimental impact on us as individuals and on those who work with us, play with us, and live with us. We might hear arrogance expressed in the following verbiage:

- "I'm clearly the best at what I do. No one else even comes close."

- "Why would I listen to their ideas? Mine are always superior."

- "I don't need help or advice from anyone. I've got everything under control."

- "I'm always right. Everyone else is just too ignorant to see it."

- "They should feel privileged to be in my presence."

- "I'm too important to waste my time on insignificant matters or people."

- "I deserve all the recognition and rewards because I'm simply better than everyone else."

- "I'm far too intelligent for this conversation. It's beneath me."

- "I don't need to apologize. It's their fault for not meeting my expectations."

When we use such phrases, we hinder genuine connections because arrogance fosters a lack of respect for others. We become more concerned with protecting our status and power positions than engaging with others. The emotion of arrogance inhibits effective communication by discouraging active listening and making open dialogue difficult. When we yield to the emotion of arrogance, we may dominate conversations, dismiss other people's opinions and ideas, interrupt others who are speaking, and encourage misunderstandings and fractured communication channels.

Our culture seems to reward arrogance, placing emphasis on self-promotion and individual achievement at all costs. In many spheres, from competitive workplaces to media platforms, there is a pervasive belief that confidence is key, even when that confidence reaches the level of arrogance. The cult of celebrity, for example, often glorifies those who exude a sense of self-importance, reinforcing the notion that arrogance equates to power and influence. This cultural reinforcement of arrogance can create a cycle where individuals strive to adopt such behaviors in order to gain recognition and validation.

In practice, however, we see the emotion of arrogance play an important role in damaging professional relationships, hindering our ability to collaborate with our colleagues, and impeding career advancement. Arrogance deals a heavy blow to our ability to grow and learn because it assumes that we know everything about a particular topic. The belief in one's superiority can create a closed mindset, hindering our willingness to consider alternative perspectives or acknowledge our own limitations or personal shortcomings. Colleagues or superiors may be disinclined to work with someone who displays arrogance, impacting opportunities for professional development and success.

When leaders in organizations succumb to arrogance, it can have far-reaching and detrimental effects on the overall health and success of the institution. It can create a culture of fear and intimidation. Arrogance can lead to poor decision-making and low morale because people feel their viewpoints are not welcomed or valued. This not only stifles innovation and creativity but also undermines trust within the organization. It can cause leaders to alienate their team members, creating a toxic work environment characterized by resentment, disengagement, and a lack of collaboration. Furthermore, the emotion of arrogance reduces the likelihood we will admit mistakes or seek help from our teams or outside consultants. This prevents the organization from learning and adapting, which hinders its long-term growth and success.

# THE IMPULSE TO JUDGE

**The more one judges, the less one loves.**

— Honore de Balzac

From each one of these emotions arises the impulse to judge yourself or others. This is what our inner critic does. When we feel shame, we are judging ourselves to be inferior to our expectations of ourselves, or the expectations we believe others have for us. When we feel entitled, we are judging circumstances as unjust and unfair with regards to our personal perceptions. When we feel arrogance, we are judging ourselves as superior to others in some manner. We are doing this in hopes of achieving some level of psychological validation in the judgment. The impulse to judge is an innate aspect of human nature. It is a cognitive process through which we evaluate and make sense of the world. Our brains are designed to sort and categorize everything that crosses our path in order to find patterns to protect and serve our interests. It involves forming opinions, making comparisons, and assessing the behaviors, choices, or characteristics of others. Judgment can serve as a useful tool for discernment and decision-making at its base level. For example, you may see a group of individuals who appear dangerous and choose to avoid their path. This could save your life.

However, the natural impulse to judge can be transformed into destructive emotions and behaviors when we assume that everything our critic tells us is true and refuse to reflect on its judgment objectively. This often leads to negative consequences when our critic is driven by bias, misconceptions, or a desire to assert superiority. Judgment will also inevitably lead back to level-three emotions when we use it to feel validated. There is always someone who has more than us and our expectations can change in any moment.

We give in to the impulse to judge based on many factors, but there are three primary reasons we judge:

- **Self-preservation:** Judgment can be a protective mechanism aimed at classifying potential threats or determining what is safe or acceptable based on our own beliefs and values. This can be negative when we prioritize self-preservation over the well-being of others or if our perceptions are misguided. We may have heard that a certain area is dangerous, and so we assume the innocent person asking for directions is trying to harm us.
- **Social comparison:** It has been said that "comparison is the thief of joy." Humans tend to compare themselves to others as a means of self-evaluation, leading to judgments based on perceived differences in status, success, or appearance. This can be positive if it inspires you to improve or negative if it triggers level-three emotions. Additionally, it could also cause you to conform to certain behaviors that are detrimental. You may have seen the experiment where a researcher stood on a sidewalk and looked up at the sky. Within moments, several others stopped to look as well, even though there was nothing unusual

happening. The same is true of the elevator experiment, where several researchers stepped onto an elevator facing the back rather than the front. Others who got on did the same. We tend to evaluate ourselves by the standard of what others are doing, thinking, or feeling, causing us to judge ourselves and others for behaving differently. This can very easily be abused by those with malintent.

**Fear and insecurity:** Judgment can be a defense mechanism that helps alleviate or feed our own insecurities by asserting superiority, devaluing others, or searching for confirmation of our negative feelings toward ourselves. Rather than celebrate the accomplishments of others, their success serves as an indictment of our failures. For example, we may intentionally look for flaws in others when they accomplish something that makes us feel insecure. This serves to preserve our self-image.

Just like with harm, when we judge others, we are also judging ourselves either directly or indirectly. There is always a frame of reference for casting judgment. This is usually our current self-image or the idealized version of ourselves that we feel like we should embody (and sometimes feel that we are, even though we are not). This always creates tension internally and externally between ourselves and others because our self-image is never exact.

## The 5 Levels of Conscience

Internally, we often feel inferior to the idealized version we build in our minds of ourselves or others. This manifests as and reinforces our feelings of shame, but it can also trigger entitlement and arrogance. Most often, it is a feeling of inferiority hidden beneath displays of entitlement and arrogance, rather than genuine feelings of superiority. In fact, many times, a genuine feeling of superiority will illicit compassion and the desire to do good for those less fortunate. This is rarely the case with inferiority. Sometimes, though, we will have genuine feelings of superiority and even seek them out in order to try and fill the gap between our current self-image and our idealized self-image. For example, bullying or belittling others. These feelings are always short-lived and rarely ever lead to any lasting benefits. More often, they will lead right back to shame.

We also generate tension externally between ourselves and others as a result of judgment because it is uncomfortable to feel judged by someone. This is true whether it is in a positive or negative light. It pulls us away from the outer world and into ourselves. This causes us to evaluate ourselves and creates distance and awkwardness because we can never know how others truly see us. It is also uncomfortable when you recognize someone is judging themselves. We are always most comfortable when we are all together in the moment as one collective consciousness. Any time that is disrupted, it is very easily felt and will always cause tension.

# ISOLATION

> **The worst cruelty that can be inflicted on a human being is isolation.**
>
> — **Sukarno**

As we touched on earlier in the chapter, the emotions of this level will manifest as isolation as you give in to your impulse to judge and take heed of your inner critic. Either we isolate ourselves intentionally because of shame to avoid the perceived judgment of others, or others isolate us because entitlement or arrogance works to push people away and sever relationships.

Acute and intentional isolation can actually be very beneficial. It gives us time and space to focus, and if we intentionally provide ourselves with something worthwhile to focus on, we can make exceptional progress in record time. However, chronic and extended isolation can be very dangerous, and we should do our best not to fall into the trap. We can recognize the patterns of isolation in the following ways:

First, there is a sense of disconnection and distance from others, both emotionally and physically. We may feel like an outsider, excluded from meaningful connections and relationships. In this manner, we will sink into our internal world, failing to participate with others in the here and now.

Second, isolation often manifests in a lack of genuine intimacy and vulnerability. We may struggle to form deep connections or fear being truly seen and understood by others. We will hide aspects of ourselves that we reject and stifle ourselves in an attempt to conform to what we believe others want us to be.

Third, isolation can result in a diminished support system. We may find ourselves lacking a network of trusted individuals who provide support, understanding, and encouragement. This will lead us further into our shells, often causing us to act in ways that seem bizarre to others. Without exposure to the energy and thought patterns of others, we may fail to recognize when our behaviors deviate too far from what is acceptable.

Fourth, isolation may manifest as a constant feeling of loneliness. We may lack healthy social interactions, which will cause us to long for someone to talk to, someone to love, or someone that understands us. On occasion, even in the presence of others, despite being surrounded by people, there is an underlying sense of being alone and misunderstood. We feel like an outsider who doesn't "belong." Remember, there is a difference between "aloneness" and "loneliness." Aloneness is the physical quality of being alone at the time, which one might enjoy. Loneliness is a state of lack and neediness that is not dependent upon being isolated from others.

Finally, isolation can be observed through a limited perspective or an inability to empathize with others. When trapped in the cycle of shame, entitlement, or arrogance, we become self-focused and fail to recognize and connect with the experiences and needs of those around us. This can also lead to abstract and absurd thinking that does not resonate with those around you.

Recognizing these signs of isolation can serve as a wake-up call, motivating us to break free from the confines of lower conscience and seek connection, empathy, and genuine relationships. If we fail to do so, this isolation, both physical and psychological, can have detrimental effects on our physical and mental health. Studies have consistently shown that isolation can increase the risk of mortality as much or more than obesity and even drug and alcohol abuse. These patterns have even been demonstrated in organisms as simple as ants. Isolation will tend to pull you downwards toward level two in the form of despair or hatred and can even cause seemingly normal people to descend into madness over extended periods. This can be particularly dangerous because, in a distorted state of awareness, it will be much more difficult to even recognize you have an issue, let alone do the difficult work required to take control of your emotions and behaviors.

## LEVEL 3 PRACTICE
# HUMILITY

> *It was pride that changed angels into devils; it is humility that makes men as angels.*
> — **Saint Augustine**

Humility is the bridge that helps us transition from a state of shame, entitlement, and arrogance to a higher level of emotional conscience and awareness. In humility, we feel connected to others and are part of one and the same Creation. We no longer need to feel separate and individually validated as we are all equal parts of one perfect whole. When we identify that we are in level three, we can take steps to embrace humility, which will challenge our negative beliefs, fostering empathy and cultivating a greater sense of self-awareness and connection with others.

This is, for many, the most difficult practice in which to engage. Our ego cannot stand to ask for forgiveness or admit our faults. This is because it wants to remain separate, unique, and distinguished from others, and whether that is in a positive or negative manner does not make a difference. It is also very difficult because, as children, many of us received love and validation from our guardians only when we behaved in certain ways. This reinforces the idea that we are only safe and loved when we are perfect. Admitting fault and imperfection is basically admitting that we are not worthy of love and safety. This can be extremely threatening to the subconscious. We also struggle to forgive others because, in that spiteful state of non-forgiveness, we feel superior to them. In humility though, we forgive them because we know that we could have done the same in their situation, and one day we may be the ones asking forgiveness.

Humility is not an admission that we are beneath others. It is the realization that we are exactly as others are. Bruce Lee famously said, when asked if he identified as American or as Chinese, "Under the sky, under the heavens, there is but one family." We are all connected. From humans, to animals, to fungi, to plants, we are all made from stardust and will eventually return to stardust. As humans, we all experience the same emotions and impulses and for any of us to judge and condemn one another accomplishes nothing productive in the long run. It only creates distance, isolation, and internal conflict. Once you fully internalize this, humility becomes your default state, as opposed to a practice.

## The 5 Levels of Conscience

### Example:

Imagine you are a college student who has just received another failing test grade on your exam. As others celebrate their scores, you experience a wave of shame wash over you as you compare yourself to your peers, feeling inadequate and humiliated. The weight of your perceived incompetence leads you to judge yourself as a failure. You start thinking about how hard you studied and conclude, "I deserved a better grade. This test must have been poorly structured. In fact, the professor is to blame. He was a poor instructor." You remember your friends in the class and feel upset that they did well when you believe you are much smarter than they are. As these feelings feed on one another, you quickly recede home into your dorm to avoid the discomfort that is caused by the presence of your fellow students. There is a fork in the road here. One person may fall lower into despair and inaction, or spite, while the other humbles themselves, approaches the professor, and asks, "How can I improve next time?" This humility removes the burden of performance, achievement, and perfection and helps you accept your humanity. You forgive yourself for not being perfect, and it spurs you to ask for the help you need to do better and to be thankful for the other places in life where you are enjoying success.

**LEVEL 3 EXERCISE**

The humility practice for moving past level-three emotions is an adaptation of the traditional Hawaiian healing practice called "ho'oponopono." It roughly translates to English as: "to make right."

1. Assume a position of relaxation, either sitting, lying, or standing, (ideally in child's pose) and place your palms together as if in prayer.
2. Close your eyes and breathe however your body wants to breathe for a few moments.
    a. During these breaths, attempt to empty your mind and let go of any rumination.
    - If you are encountering resistance, bring yourself back to your senses by noting things that you can hear, feel, or smell in this moment.
    - You can also use the phrase "I wonder what my next thought will be." You'll find this helps to create space.
3. Once you find a bit of space, focus entirely on your breath as you take deep breaths in and consciously relax every inch of your body and mind as you exhale. Try to relax slightly deeper with each breath you take.
4. As you exhale, you will go through the following four phrases in your mind.
    - I am sorry
    - Please forgive me

# The 5 Levels of Conscience

- **Thank you**

- **I love you**

You can also use more specific language. "I am sorry for _____". "Please forgive me for _____". "I forgive myself for _____". You may be asking forgiveness from someone in particular or asking forgiveness of yourself. As always, the important thing is to *feel* a sense of humility and connectedness with all things. Feel free to also add in other phrases that help to cultivate a sense of humility such as:

- "I cannot know everything."

- "I am one instance of an interconnected universe."

- "It feels great to be a part of one beautiful wholeness."

- "I am imperfect in so many ways, and that is okay because so are others."

- "Please give me the strength to move past these obstacles."

Finally, you can also choose to send love and appreciation to everyone and everything you can think of. This practice helps to reinforce the connection and sameness of all things.

Additionally, here are some practices you can use to avoid falling into level-three emotions in the first place:

- **Connect with Nature:** Nothing will help to permanently integrate humility more than to truly realize that all living beings are interconnected as one. Every time you see another living being, think of them as a brother or sister. Speak to them and acknowledge them as you would your kin. You can even practice this with plants. Place your hand on a tree and tell it that you love it and would not be alive without it. If you can do this without shame, you will have mastered humility in that moment.

- **Ask Questions:** Ask questions more than you make statements. Asking a question is a surefire way to show others that you value them. Actively seek input, listen attentively, and consider different viewpoints with an open mind. Use feedback as an opportunity for growth and learning. Remember that any of the lower-level emotions can be rooted in anger. So, especially when you are feeling angry, stopping long enough to ask a question can abate the answer and open space for understanding. Of course, asking is useless without active listening. Active listening means dismissing the urge to formulate your response while the other person is speaking. It suggests that you want to hear them rather than waiting for your turn to speak. It means nodding when you agree and understand or asking, "Can you say more about that?" when

## The 5 Levels of Conscience

you do not. Pausing after a person finishes speaking is a powerful active listening tool because it gives you time to truly consider their words. Stephen Covey once suggested, "Seek first to understand, then to be understood."

— **Check Your Gratitude**: When our inner critic tells us that we are superior or that someone else is repulsive, we can check back to our level of gratitude and remember that there are an infinite number of uncontrollable circumstances that could have led us to be in a situation exactly as the person we are judging. Remember the proverb: "There, but for the grace of God (our Creator), go I."

— **Cultivate Empathy**: Develop empathy by putting yourself in others' shoes, actively listening, and seeking to understand their experiences and perspectives. Treat others with kindness, respect, and compassion. This can start with something as simple as cultivating new responses, such as:

- "I appreciate your feedback and will consider it."

- I'm grateful for the opportunity to learn from others."

- "I don't have all the answers, but I'm open to different perspectives."

- "I'm sorry if my actions caused any harm. I'll do better next time."

- "I'm fortunate to have had supportive people in my life."

- "I value the contributions of others in this team/project."

- "I'm still a work in progress, constantly learning and growing."

- "I'm grateful for the chance to collaborate with such talented individuals."

- "I'm happy to help; no task is beneath me."

- "I believe in giving credit where it's due; others played a significant role in our success."

— **Embrace Lifelong Learning**: Adopt a mindset of continuous learning and growth. Recognize that knowledge is vast, and there is always more to discover. Stay curious, ask questions, and remain open to new ideas. Read often and participate in discussion groups. Do so with an open mind to see what you can learn that you didn't know before. When you encourage feedback, you lift yourself from level three with a mindset that welcomes growth. Encourage others to provide constructive criticism and listen attentively when it's offered. Resist defensiveness or a need to justify your actions.

— **Practice Humble Confidence**: Often, the error people make is assuming that humility and confidence cannot coexist. They can and do. Embrace a humble form of self-assurance. Recognize your strengths and accomplishments without needing to assert superiority over others. Share credit and acknowledge the contributions of those around you. Acknowledge and appreciate the contributions of others in your team, community, or personal relationships. Highlight the strengths and achievements of others rather than solely focusing on your own. Consider a ratio of 1:1. For example, you might say, "I am so happy that I gave an amazing performance." Then add, "I could not have done it without the incredible people who are so great at their jobs and make my job easy."

**Practice Humble Service:** Engage in acts of service or volunteering without seeking recognition or praise. Do these secretly without telling anyone. Humble service involves offering your time, skills, or resources to help others without expecting anything in return. This exercise fosters a sense of humility by focusing on the needs of others.

## WHY IT WORKS

Fundamental to all aspects of level three is a sense of separateness and differentiation from others. Humility is the antithesis of level-three emotions because it is a virtue rooted in a profound sense of interconnectedness with others and with Creation. It is impossible to feel invalidated if we are all equally part of one perfect whole. We can only feel invalidated if we are different, separate, and judged to be less than.

Humility functions through an increased self-awareness and an acknowledgment of one's limitations, imperfections, and the fact that we share those same imperfections and limitations with others. It is not about self-deprecation or diminishing your own worth. Instead, it centers around an honest acknowledgment of our strengths and weaknesses without needing to assert superiority or dominance. Humility allows us to approach life with a sense of curiosity, empathy, and a genuine desire to learn from others, understanding that our shared experiences are beneficial and often necessary to create a well-rounded life.

Humility is the antidote to shame because part of shame is the idea that we should be something more or better than we are. Humility says we are exactly as others are and there is no point in even entertaining the idea of more or better. When shame arises from trauma, as in the case where we have been victimized, shame is our way of saying we caused the trauma or should have been able to stop it somehow. Humility says the opposite. It suggests that we are often powerless to protect ourselves and have to deal with the malevolent acts of others who are operating on lower levels of conscience. Despite this fact, we are no different from them and no better or worse for having gone through that trauma. It also teaches us to admit that, although we are imperfect, we are always capable of learning, growing, and strengthening our minds, spirits, and bodies. Humility encourages us to practice self-forgiveness, let go of the weight of shame, and embrace a mindset that promotes self-compassion, understanding, and acceptance both for ourselves and for others. In the final stages of healing trauma, you'll be able to integrate the idea that, on another timeline, you could have been the offender. We are all capable of all behaviors and emotions. Remember, "There, but for the grace of God (our Creator), go I." This can be a very difficult concept to accept when someone else has done horrific things, but to think that we are incapable of any specific act is itself a form of arrogance.

Humility will also act as a counterbalance to entitlement by reminding us of our interconnectedness and the inherent dignity and worth of every individual. By cultivating humility, we recognize that our achievements are not solely due to our own efforts. They are often supported by the contributions of many. We also recognize that our needs and wants are no more important than anyone else's and that, while we may excel in certain domains, we do not excel in all domains.

Finally, humility serves as an effective tool to combat arrogance by fostering empathy, openness, and a willingness to learn from others. When we embrace humility, we acknowledge that our own knowledge, abilities, and experiences are limited in a limitless universe. Eventually, we all must rely on others in some manner to achieve true fulfillment rather than by asserting dominance in an attempt to temporarily satisfy a self-interested impulse.

Ultimately, humility will place our self-image and self-awareness on the same level as others. It allows us infinite space to forgive ourselves and to forgive others. From this perspective, you will naturally begin to feel the emotions and impulses from levels four and five, and the toxicity in your life will diminish quickly and drastically.

## WHAT TO EXPECT

Humble individuals are more inclined to listen actively and empathize with others, fostering stronger connections and healthier relationships. Moreover, practicing humility helps us move away from negative emotions as we let go of the need to be right all the time and practice being open to constructive criticism. We can also expect an improved capacity for self-reflection and a deeper understanding of our own strengths and weaknesses. As a result, humility often leads to increased resilience and adaptability that enables us to face challenges with a more balanced approach. You'll find that you begin to improve in ways you never even noticed you could use improvement and at rates you aren't accustomed to.

Humility will open many new perspectives for you that dissipate judgmental thoughts of yourself and others. Something that once triggered intense shame and insecurity is now something to laugh about because you don't take yourself so seriously. Another thing that once caused you to look down on others will now be the reason why you want to help them.

Additionally, humility is contagious. When others witness this virtue in action, they are inspired to cultivate it themselves, creating a positive ripple effect in both personal and professional spheres. You will find that you are more freely able to be your authentic self, becoming infinitely more attractive and secure as you inspire others to do the same. This will cause a magnetic attraction where others cannot help but to move into your orbit. Overall, practicing humility leads to greater self-awareness, improved relationships, and a more harmonious and empathetic engagement with people and Creation.

Your resistance will tell you, "I can't forgive myself. This damage is permanent." Or "But I *am* better than them; what good does it do to delude myself?" As you move past these delusions, ask for forgiveness, and embrace your imperfections willfully, your ego begins to fade and the resistance will subside.

*Luis Ali*

As we begin to feel a sense of humility, we cultivate a receptive mindset and maintain our youthful curiosity. It helps us acknowledge that we need others just as they need us because we learn from different perspectives. It also serves to align us with the natural flow and order of Creation instead of resisting the tides in an attempt to distinguish ourselves. While asking for forgiveness can be one of the most difficult tasks to do as it involves admitting our own flaws or wrongdoings, the beautiful part is that forgiveness is infinite, and no matter what has happened there is always the ability to be forgiven by yourself, by others, and by our Creator.

*The 5 Levels of Conscience*

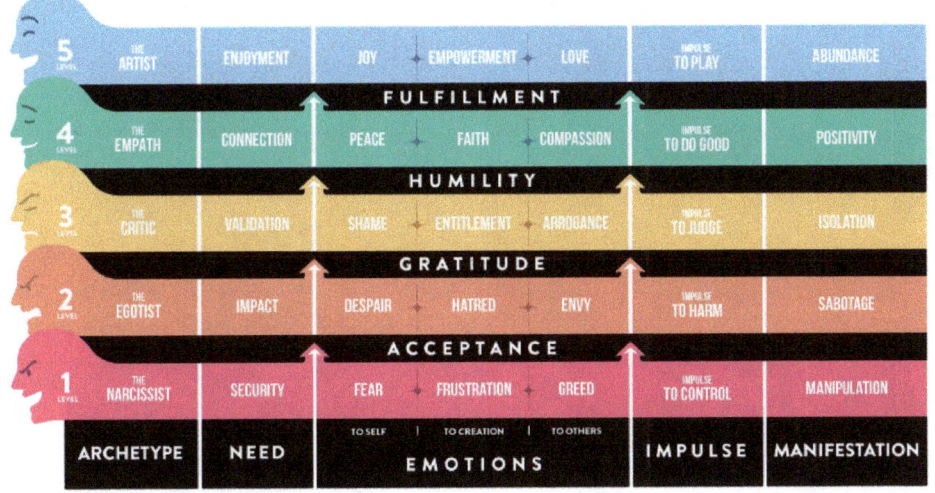

# LEVEL 4: THE EMPATH

Jane Addams was born in 1860 to a prosperous family in Illinois. As a child, she suffered from tuberculosis of the spine, which led to lifelong health issues. Despite the hardship, Addams was inspired to do something great for the world and decided she would become a doctor so that she could help alleviate the suffering of the poor and the sick.

She was one of the first wave of women in the country to receive a college education, excelling in all aspects and graduating from Rockford Female Seminary in 1881. However, under the immense pressure to help others and her lifelong health problems, she suffered a nervous breakdown that prevented her from completing the degree, shattering her dream.

She fell into a deep despair yet continued to develop herself through reading and travel. One day, while reading a magazine, she learned about, and later visited, the world's first settlement house,

Toynbee Hall, in London. Inspired by the great work they were doing, she realized that she didn't have to become a doctor to help others and, eventually, she established her own Hull House in Chicago.

Hull House became a center of support for the community, including a daycare for working mothers, educational programs for adults and children, job training, and a space for cultural exchange. It later became a research center for social reform, attracting intellectuals, artists, and social workers who shared Addams' vision of a more just and equitable society.

In 1931, Addams became the first American woman to be awarded the Nobel Peace Prize. Her story demonstrates the toll our desire to do good can have on our health, and the great things that come when we let go of that desire and focus on the things that bring us fulfillment instead.

## THE EMPATH

> **When you show deep empathy toward others, their defensive energy goes down, and positive energy replaces it.**
> **— Stephen Covey**

The archetype of level four is the empath. The empath has many positive characteristics and can attract a lot of people and positivity into their lives. They are great at understanding others, recognizing their emotions, and are very generous in their impulses to do good for those around them. This is certain to generate strong relationships and success. However, there are a few downsides to the archetype. While empaths will attract love and positivity, they will also attract toxic people, particularly narcissists, who are looking to abuse their generous nature. This can lead to physical, emotional, and spiritual exhaustion, as well as catastrophic relationships. Many times, an empath's attempts and desires to heal others are a subtle cry for help and contain within them a subconscious request to be healed themselves. The beautiful thing is that this healing happens from within, without the help of others, and can be experienced instantaneously through fulfillment.

It is worth reiterating that just as the lower emotions do not define us, neither do the higher ones. None of us are any one thing all the time. At any given moment, and with the right stimulus, we can all find ourselves anywhere on the chart. It is important to remember that we operate from a place of acceptance of who we are, noticing the emotions we are feeling and then reaching for a higher emotional level by evaluating our connection to self, Creation, and others.

Remember that the higher we go on the scale, the less desire we have for change and the less we resist what is. The lower we go, the greater lengths we will go to try to force change and cause stress and damage in the process. On level four, we have a calm acceptance of life, along with a sense of gratitude and a humble connection to others, but *something* is still missing. As stated in the introduction, the highest level we can achieve is when there is no desire to change anything because we are living in full enjoyment of the present moment.

## CONNECTION

> Your connections to all the things around you literally define who you are.
>
> — Aaron D. O'Connell

Connection with others is one of the great gifts that we have in our human experience. Our ancestors who formed strong social bonds with others were more likely to survive and reproduce by sharing resources, as well as by protecting and supporting each other. This allowed us to begin to specialize our abilities because we could rely on others for things at which we did not personally excel. Things like trust and reliability were emphasized and we began to form large groups of cohesive societies with specialized skills. This wired our brains to crave connection and brought about our abilities to sense each other's thoughts and emotions through mirror neurons. This was the beginning of our capacity for empathy.

## The 5 Levels of Conscience

Having people to share our thoughts, feelings, actions, and opinions with helps to foster a sense of belonging. It allows us to connect with things that are greater than just ourselves and align with specific values and movements that we care about. These feelings of connection and belonging are what encourage us to help others and further support us in our endeavors to cooperate and effect positive change in the world. It's been said that happiness is only real when shared. Connection provides the means by which we can create and share happiness with those around us. It also encourages us to share our vulnerabilities. This is key to forming deep bonds that come before any personal interests.

There are some ways that this desire for connection can be destructive, however. When we form deep bonds with others, we open ourselves up to the vulnerability of them betraying us. This can be deeply traumatic and even cause people to permanently shut down to the idea of connecting with others again. Our desires for connection, belonging, and empathy can sometimes override our sense of self-trust and logic. It is not uncommon for particularly empathetic people to "sacrifice" for others and forego their personal boundaries, believing this is the highest moral good. This can eventually lead to burnout, strained relationships, and a reflexive submission to others where we do not set boundaries or stand up for ourselves. Additionally, when we are particularly lonely, lost, or in vulnerable situations, we can end up joining groups or movements that are toxic. This is the manner in which most famous cult leaders prey on people. The connection these groups provide can be intoxicating and becomes an easy way to manipulate people into behaving in destructive manners. We don't even have to go as far as to join a cult to fall into this pattern. Feeling a strong connection to any group, whether it is a political party, a sports team, or even a corporate brand, can override our logical mind. The next thing we know, we are committing violence, ignoring our better judgment, and reflexively going along with anything the group decides for us.

Being caught in a toxic cycle on level four can be destructive, but the great news is that, with just a small shift in perspective, you can quickly make your way into level five. Many people almost never make it to level four but for fleeting moments, so don't worry. When you recognize you might be in the cycle, just ask yourself:

- "Am I sacrificing anything for this group or relationship in a way that is not conducive to my well-being?"
- "Is this group or relationship contributing to my fulfillment and enjoyment or draining it?"
- "Is this a mutually beneficial scenario, or am I giving more than I am receiving?"
- "Could both parties amicably walk away from this connection, or would either side have an excessively negative reaction?"
- "Is the other party being harmed by this relationship in any way?"

## The 5 Levels of Conscience

Our connections with others are one of life's greatest gifts. Along with our memories and our freedom of thought, they are one of the few things that no one can fully take away from us. Connection is one of our greatest tools in learning, achievement, and overall enjoyment of life. With these few simple reflections, we can ensure that our connections are healthy and we are reaping the benefits of this gift.

## PEACE

> **If you are depressed you are living in the past if you are anxious you are living in the future. If you are at peace, you are living in the present.**
> — Lao Tzu

In our increasingly interconnected and demanding world, finding peace has become increasingly difficult. Peace refers to that state of tranquility and harmony within oneself. It is a sanctuary where one can find solace and balance in spite of the chaos of life.

As is the case with every emotion we have explored, peace is not a static state. Even the most even-tempered among us can sometimes find that their peace is disturbed as they slide down the levels of conscience. This can be exacerbated when our empathic tendencies pull us into the chaos of others. Peace is a dynamic process that requires conscious effort and introspection. But it doesn't have to be difficult. It begins with self-awareness and aligning our thoughts, emotions, and actions in a way that promotes harmony within ourselves.

Peace might be described as:

- Relief
- Relaxation
- Harmony
- Tranquility
- Serenity
- Calmness
- Repose
- Stillness
- Contentment
- Balance
- Reconciliation
- Unity
- Amity
- Solace

While you may appear perfectly calm and put together on the outside, true peace is measured by becoming aware of the incessant chatter within our minds. Our thoughts often wander aimlessly, dwelling on the past or worrying about the future. Observing our thoughts and actions without judgment or attachment helps us to cultivate inner peace. By recognizing the patterns and tendencies of our thinking, we can consciously choose to let go of negative or self-defeating thoughts

## The 5 Levels of Conscience

and replace them with positive and affirming ones. As with any new skill, this takes time and practice.

You might learn to say:

- "I am content with who I am."
- "I feel a deep sense of inner calm."
- "I embrace the present moment with gratitude."
- "I choose love and compassion over anger and resentment."
- "I find joy in the simple pleasures of life."
- "I am at peace with the past and have let go of regrets."
- "I trust in the natural flow of life and surrender to its rhythms."
- "I see the beauty and interconnectedness of all things."
- "I choose to focus on what brings me peace and let go of what doesn't."
- "I am grounded and centered in my being."

Peace is less about acquiring something and more about letting go. If you treat it as a goal to be achieved, it will elude you. Peace can also elude us when we are clinging to attachments, whether they are material possessions, relationships, or expectations. Expectations, in particular, are an enemy of peacefulness. Having expectations can create a constant state of striving and attachment to the future. When we hold expectations, we set specific conditions for our happiness and well-being. This includes goals and aspirations we expect to achieve. When those conditions are not met, we feel that we cannot relax or let go. We fixate on how things *should* be rather than embracing how they actually are. This resistance to reality creates a perpetual cycle of disappointment and frustration, pulling us into lower levels of conscience and preventing us from realizing our peace. Letting go of expectations releases us from many of the cycles that pull us into lower levels of conscience, opening the door to a deeper sense of peace. You do not have to let go of the goal or aspiration, just the *expectation* that they *will* be achieved.

By embracing the present moment, we create space for serenity and contentment to flourish within us. By cultivating a mindset of non-attachment, we free ourselves from the burden of craving and clinging. This doesn't mean we should avoid or reject the joys of life and never work toward goals. What it does mean is that there must be a balance where we develop a healthy detachment and an understanding that nothing is permanent, and that true peace comes from within. This allows us to approach our goals with a clear mind and conscience that encourages fulfillment regardless of the outcome.

# FAITH

> **To one who has faith, no explanation is necessary. To one without faith, no explanation is possible.**
>
> **— Thomas Aquinas**

Faith, in its essence, is a deep-seated belief and trust in either ourselves, something greater than ourselves, or both in harmony. It is a fundamental aspect of the human experience that we rely on for solace, guidance, and hope, especially in times of uncertainty. Without it, we are more easily knocked off course and more subject to the negative energies that bring us down.

Faith is often connected to religion. This is because religion is an ideal framework for looking beyond the self toward something else that we deem to be higher and more virtuous. But faith can operate inside or outside of religious boundaries. It encompasses a broader idea of trust, beliefs, values, and conviction in our Creator. It offers a lens through which we make sense of the world, find meaning in adversity, and find the strength to navigate the uncertainties of life.

Faith plays a vital role in personal growth and development. It feels warm and comforting and helps give us the courage to continue to press on in light of setbacks and obstacles. It offers a sense of direction, anchoring us in an ever-changing world. We often hear faith referred to as:

- Belief
- Trust
- Conviction
- Determination
- Hope
- Assurance
- Reliance
- Devotion
- Loyalty
- Allegiance
- Courage
- Honor

While faith is sometimes expressed outwardly toward a greater power or set of values, we can also have faith in ourselves. As we grow in self-confidence, resilience, and wisdom, the faith we have in ourselves encourages us to pursue our dreams and overcome obstacles. It fuels our motivation and propels us toward our potential because we feel we can trust that the outcome of our endeavors will be positive regardless of the setbacks along the way.

Faith is not limited to an individual's personal journey. Faith is also expressed well in community and in relationships with others. Though our culture often seeks to convince us to trust no one, on a higher level of conscience we learn to trust in the inherent goodness of others while accepting and acknowledging that we are all flawed.

Trust and faith are intertwined, forming the bedrock of strong and healthy connections. When we have faith in others, we build deeper bonds and create an environment of mutual support and understanding. We trust that the intentions of others are genuine and believe in their potential for growth and change, which fosters compassion and empathy. This kind of faith, however, must be expressed in conjunction with a forgiving attitude. People fail us just as we fail them. Through faith, we more readily extend forgiveness to others, considering our own tendency to disappoint those who are counting on us.

Moreover, faith in relationships goes beyond human connections. It extends to the faith we have in the resilience and strength of our values, such as faith in love, faith in radical honesty, or faith in goodness itself. In times of conflict or hardship, faith becomes the guiding force that helps us work through challenges, nurture understanding, and build trust. It reminds us that relationships are dynamic and capable of healing and growth.

Faith also fosters a positive mindset, helping us cultivate hope and a more optimistic outlook. Believing in the possibility of a brighter future or the potential for change empowers us to persevere in the face of setbacks. It allows us to view challenges as opportunities for growth and learning, rather than as insurmountable barriers.

That is why you often hear people who experience this emotion say things like:

- "I trust that everything happens for a reason."
- "I have faith in the goodness of humanity."
- "I believe in the power of love and compassion to create positive change."
- "I find strength in my faith during times of adversity."
- "I have confidence in my abilities and know that I can overcome any challenges."
- "I trust in the divine plan and surrender to the flow of life."
- "I have faith that justice will prevail, and truth will triumph."
- "I believe that miracles can happen if we open our hearts and minds."
- "I trust in the process of healing and growth, both for myself and others."
- "I have faith that my efforts and actions make a difference in the world."
- "I know our Creator wants what is best for me."
- "Our Creator wants me to succeed."

## The 5 Levels of Conscience

Sometimes, your faith will be challenged. You will see someone exhibit lower-level behaviors and to seemingly "get away with it." You may also experience the phenomenon of "no good deed goes unpunished," or you may see someone lie, cheat, and manipulate their way to monetary riches. In these times, it is important to remember that, in our limited perspective, we cannot see the entire picture and there are likely forces at play that will correct any perceived disruption in these patterns. It is also important to note that anything gained out of lower-level behaviors is not worth having and comes with negative internal consequences that are not readily apparent from the outside. For example, an executive who makes it to the top of an organization through manipulative tactics will generally be despised by their peers and be left with no one to trust and no one to enjoy their success with.

Faith serves as a powerful tool in cultivating resilience. It acts like a life preserver, preventing us from falling into negative emotions, and allowing us to bounce back from adversity and find meaning in difficult circumstances. It provides comfort and solace during times of loss or uncertainty that may otherwise lead to toxicity. It instills in us the belief that challenges are temporary and that there is a larger tapestry at play beyond our immediate understanding.

# COMPASSION

> **If you want others to be happy, practice compassion. If you want to be happy, practice compassion.**
>
> **— Dalai Lama**

Compassion stems from the ability to empathize with the suffering of others. But it goes beyond just a feeling. Compassion motivates action. When we feel this emotion, we have a desire to alleviate the suffering we see. It goes beyond sympathy or pity and involves a deep sense of understanding and connection with others. It is about recognizing the inherent worth and dignity of every human being, regardless of their background or circumstances. That is why it sparks acts of kindness, empathy, selflessness, and an urge to alleviate the physical, emotional, and spiritual suffering of others. This is what we most commonly think of when we hear the words empath or empathy.

Compassion has a remarkable ripple effect. When we extend compassion to others, it often creates a positive chain reaction, inspiring and motivating others to do the same. A compassionate act not only helps the recipient, but also cultivates a culture of empathy and care within communities.

Compassion in our personal relationships has the power to heal and mend breaches that are inadvertently caused between us and others. Approaching conflicts and differences with compassion allows us to see the humanity in others and find common ground. Compassion fosters understanding, forgiveness, and reconciliation, paving the way for deeper connections and fostering a more harmonious society.

When we are flowing in the emotion of compassion, we might show it through:

- Empathy
- Kindness
- Sympathy
- Benevolence
- Caring
- Humanity
- Generosity
- Consideration
- Tenderness
- Mercy

We might show compassion by doing good work. Perhaps we volunteer at a food drive, collect school supplies for underprivileged children, or go the extra mile and fly to Haiti to help with cleanup and care for people after a hurricane. The sight of a smiling person in need receiving your gifts cannot help but fill you with a profound sense of joy and fulfillment. Ultimately, having compassion allows us to accept ourselves and others despite our flaws and to be vulnerable. This inspires others to reciprocate and helps you build deep, meaningful relationships instead of shallow, transactional ones.

You can recognize the emotion of compassion when you hear yourself or others say:

- "How can I help you?"

- "I understand what you're going through, and I'm here for you."

- "I'm sorry for your pain. Is there anything I can do to support you?"

- "You are not alone. I'll stand by your side through this."

- "I see your strengths and resilience, even in the midst of your challenges."

- "Your well-being matters to me. Let's find a solution together."

- "I believe in your potential and know you have the strength to overcome this."

- "I'm listening. Take all the time you need to share your thoughts and feelings."

- "I appreciate your perspective, and I'm committed to understanding you better."

# The 5 Levels of Conscience

- *"Your feelings are valid, and I want to create a safe space for you to express them."*

Where many of us struggle is with the issue of self-compassion. While some of us do well in extending compassion to others, those same people may treat themselves with harsh self-criticism when their expectations of themselves are not met. But true compassion starts within. Before we extend compassion to others, it is crucial to cultivate self-compassion. Otherwise, we are attempting to fill others from an empty cup. This can quickly lead to burnout and exhaustion. Self-compassion involves treating ourselves with kindness, understanding, and acceptance. It means acknowledging our own suffering and extending to ourselves the same care and empathy we offer others. Because it is only by accepting our own need for compassion that we can offer it to others more fully.

Remember not to let your compassion suck you into the toxicity of others. It is impossible for us to do good for everyone and there are people who are so far entrenched in negativity that you can do nothing for them. They will only drag you down as well. This can be difficult if someone you love is trapped in a self-destructive cycle. The best you can do is offer your help and nudge them in the right direction, but the ultimate choice is theirs. That is the unfortunate downside to our autonomy. Protect your own energy and keep faith that it will all work out for the best.

## LEVEL 4 IMPULSE
## THE IMPULSE TO DO GOOD

> **Those who are happiest are those who do the most for others.**
>
> — **Booker T. Washington**

The impulse to do good is an innate and powerful force rooted in compassion, empathy, honor, and a desire to connect with others in a positive manner. It is a driving force behind countless acts of kindness, generosity, and selflessness that create a ripple effect of goodness in the world. When we experience the joy and fulfillment that comes from lifting others up, we tap into a wellspring of happiness within ourselves that pulls us toward the highest level of conscience. The impulse to do good often transcends boundaries of culture, race, and beliefs, uniting humanity through shared values of care and concern for one another.

Acts of kindness abound in our world. Though we often feel a sense of despair and anxiety when consuming news reports, we must remember that these acts of kindness are not as salacious and, therefore, do not get reported as often. People may be performing acts of kindness, both large and small, all the time without calling attention to it. Helping someone carry their groceries, holding the door for a stranger, or offering a listening ear to a friend in need are all acts that stem from a genuine intention to make a positive difference in someone's day or life.

Volunteering is another way people react to their impulse to do good and is a great tool for moving us up to level five. Similarly, people satisfy their urge to do good by donating money to philanthropic endeavors. They may donate money or resources to charitable organizations that address various social issues and help those in need. Philanthropy enables individuals to support causes they are passionate about and to make a positive impact on a larger scale.

One reason many people get involved with protecting and preserving the environment through recycling, reducing waste, conserving energy, supporting sustainable practices, and advocating for environmental conservation is to ensure a healthier planet for future generations. That is the act of doing good for people who aren't even alive yet. They say a society grows strong when men plant trees whose shade they'll never experience.

Lastly, the impulse to do good can manifest through inspiring and motivating others. We mentor, train, and teach with the goal of passing on something of value to someone else and creating positivity in their lives. We also seem to enjoy both hearing and sharing stories because they ignite the spark of human connection even more.

As you think about the emotions of level four, you might consider them to be so virtuous that they are nearly unattainable. But remember, we all move up and down on the levels of conscience. Just as you might find yourself in the emotion of shame, you can find yourself on the higher level of peace, faith, and compassion with one simple exercise.

Please also remember that in excess, the consistent doing of good for others can have negative consequences. Many times, those operating on lower levels of conscience, you and I included, will take advantage of others. Those same people may think that we appear weak. Relationships can become one-sided and deteriorate. If this is the case, it is important that we don't let these situations bring us down. Our inner empath may tell us not to give up on someone.

We see ourselves in their shoes and watch us abandon ourselves in a way. This is how the impulse to do good can become pathological, draining our happiness, causing us to lose our sense of self, and cultivating deep resentment towards those for whom we are doing good.

Remember, we can never force someone to change without their cooperation, and our absence may even be the catalyst that sparks the desire within them to change. Or maybe they will never change, and we should not burden ourselves with their problems. Either way, we can recognize with a calm sense of faith that all things are happening for the greater good. We are being pulled away from people and situations that do not align with our well-being and being pulled toward the ones that do. These situations can also serve as a reminder for us not to fall into lower-level behaviors and harm others in similar ways.

Also, keep in mind that we don't always do good for others from a place of peace, faith, and compassion. Many times, we are operating with ulterior motives. We may be doing this in an attempt to gain karmic favor: "I give so much to those in need that I *deserve* to have the things I want" *(Manipulative Greed & Entitlement)*. Or perhaps we are doing good because we think the other party now owes us a favor: "If I buy them this gift, they are obligated to return romantic favors" *(Manipulative Greed & Lust)*.

Another common tactic is a passive-aggressive attempt to get a partner to change their behavior when we are too afraid of the vulnerability required to confront the issue directly: "If I clean up after their mess, they will feel shame and finally start fixing some things around the house" *(Manipulative Fear & Frustration)*. This can be a very insidious cycle because everyone may love our giving nature so much, they neither want us to change, nor notice our life force being drained away. This pattern can lead to very serious mental and physical issues, so it is important to recognize if we are being drained and exert boundaries with peaceful confidence.

Our inner empath may also conflate the idea of "feeling bad for others" as an act of goodness in and of itself. The problem is that the body does not know the difference between feeling bad on behalf of someone else or on behalf of yourself. It just recognizes the negative emotions and will respond accordingly. In addition, the negative emotions we feel on behalf of others do no good unless they inspire us to act.

By themselves, they are destructive. This is the difference between Empathy and Sympathy. Empathy recognizes others' emotions and acts accordingly. Sympathy causes us to feel other peoples' emotions even if it not beneficial for us to do so.

Sometimes, we may even condemn others for not feeling the way we do about something. We might say, "You should be appalled at their behavior!" implying that, by not feeling the same way I am feeling, that means you are bad and I am good. This is actually just arrogance and judgment seeking a feeling of superiority.

There is also the impulse to do good for others, only so that we can either feel, or appear, superior to others. This is a common form of manipulative greed known as "virtue signaling." We've all seen people recording themselves give to the homeless in order to share the video in an attempt to gain favor.

The reason we find this behavior detestable is that we realize that the motivation behind the action is inherently manipulative, and none of us can stand to be manipulated. This behavior is toxic because it will keep us trapped in lower levels of conscience because we aren't able to recognize the true emotion that lies beneath the act of kindness.

The question to ask ourselves in order to distinguish between a genuine impulse to do good and a pathological impulse is: "Am I doing this act without expecting anything in return from anyone?" If the answer is yes, your intentions are pure, and you are on level four.

# POSITIVITY

> Even
> After
> All this time
> The Sun never says to the Earth
> 'You owe me.'
> Look
> What happens
> With a love like that;
> It lights the whole sky.
> — Hafiz

There are those who believe that the impulse to do good is hard-wired in the human brain. Without it, it is hard to imagine how the human race could survive. There are also some people who strongly believe that humans, at their core, are evil. It is hard to judge someone for this opinion because of all the horrific behaviors humans are capable of and continue to exhibit on a daily basis. However, I believe that humans are inherently good for two reasons. The first is because this perspective, in and of itself, is healthier and attracts more positivity in one's life. We tend to find the things and attract the things we look for; thus, believing in the positive nature of humanity will help us find it more often. The second is because when you compare people who exhibit negative emotions and behaviors consistently to the people who exhibit positive emotions and behaviors consistently, you will see that those who are the most negative tend to look unhealthy and age faster, while the ones who are the most positive tend to live longer and healthier lives. This is our Creator's way of limiting lower-level behaviors and encouraging the higher ones.

Doing good for others not only helps to support your consistent stay in the higher levels of conscience but also tends to manifest as general positive outcomes in your life. In healthy doses, and coming from the emotions of level four, you gain an increasing sense of well-being and fulfillment that will naturally pull you upward toward level five. People will begin to respect and love you more and want to reciprocate the good you've done for them in ways you'll never expect. Life becomes more synchronous. Certain people who do not have your best interest in mind will begin to reveal themselves and their intentions. While those who do will begin to align themselves stronger than ever before.

Adopting a positive outlook can have a major impact on your physical and mental well-being. Positive emotions, like happiness, gratitude, and love, are associated with feelings of pleasure and contentment that contribute to health and longevity. But the magic of positivity is that it has a ripple effect that extends beyond us. A single act of kindness or a genuine smile can create a chain reaction, inspiring others to do the same for others. As individuals radiate positivity, they contribute to creating a more supportive and compassionate community.

Also, as a result of your peace, faith, and compassion, you will be more able to see the silver lining in seemingly negative circumstances. Feelings of frustration, despair, and judgment won't arise as often because your intrinsic reaction to negativity will be to accept the situation and have faith in the yet unmanifested positivity.

A positive mindset equips us with the resilience to weather storms with unwavering determination. Instead of dwelling on failures, we view challenges as opportunities for growth and learning. Our setbacks are not permanent but are followed by a hopefulness that we can do better. The power of positivity allows us to bounce back from setbacks armed with inner strength and a deeper understanding of our capabilities.

With this in mind, however, it is important not to fall into the trap of believing that everything *has* to be positive all the time and to self-deprecate when you do feel sad or frustrated. This can lead to you ignoring situations that *do* need to change, like a toxic friendship or career. This is actually the impulse to control in disguise. When you feel any of the lower-level emotions, please do not judge yourself. Just catch yourself and follow the chart back up at your natural pace.

## LEVEL 4 PRACTICE — FULFILLMENT

> If you look to others for fulfillment, you will never be fulfilled. If your happiness depends on money, you will never be happy with yourself. Be content with that you have; rejoice in the way things are. When you realize there is nothing lacking, the world belongs to you.
>
> — Lao Tzu

You can take active steps to reach level five by aiming for feelings of fulfillment. Fulfillment is a pervasive sense of contentment and approval that comes when we are fully present, living in alignment with our values and passions. In fulfillment, you no longer seek to change anything because everything is as it should be. You fully approve of yourself, of Creation, and of others. It is a state of being that goes beyond momentary pleasure. It taps into the infinite joy that may lie dormant inside us.

When we grow, contribute to society, and find joy in meaningful self-expression, we feel more fulfilled because we are engaging in activities and pursuits that align with our authentic selves.

This differs greatly from the temporary satisfaction that comes from satiating our desires. This satisfaction is short-lived and will always require another desire to be satiated. This sends us in endless loops that become increasingly difficult to satisfy, while fulfillment can be achieved at any moment, for any length of time, and does not depend on anything else outside of ourselves.

A crucial aspect of fulfillment lies in discovering and embracing our unique talents and gifts. This involves exploring our values and passions and aligning them with our actions and life choices. This includes things like our hobbies, culture, history, and other endeavors that spark our imagination and ignite our inner fire. By uncovering what truly matters to us and connecting with an intention that resonates deeply, we create a foundation for a fulfilling life.

That said, fulfillment is also wrapped in our human connections. Meaningful connections and nourishing relationships are vital contributors to our sense of fulfillment. Cultivating supportive, loving, and authentic relationships, whether with family, friends, romantic partners, or communities, provides a sense of belonging, connection, and emotional fulfillment.

Ultimately, the final key is that in a state of complete fulfillment, you will naturally let go of the desire for anything to be different from the way it is currently, the way it was before, and the way it will naturally unfold in the future.

## *The 5 Levels of Conscience*

## Example:

Imagine it's a beautiful sunny day. You notice the weather is perfect as you are driving to the park to enjoy yourself. You are relaxed and certain it will be a great day. Then you notice the tent city as you pass along the bridge leading to the park. You can't help but feel sorry for them and notice the shame they must feel and the filthy conditions they must endure. You feel you must do something, but what? You spend the remainder of the drive thinking about how our society got to this state and why there aren't more support systems. You are halfway through your time at the park when you realize, "Wow, I've spent a lot of energy and paid almost no attention to this beautiful scenery." You decide that you will schedule a time to volunteer at a later date as you breathe deeply into the present moment, focusing on the fulfilling aspects of your life. That's enough. Nothing else needs to change in this moment as you enjoy the warmth of the sun on your skin.

This simple exercise will help you move up to the highest level of conscience when you realize you are on level four:

1. In any position of relaxation, sitting, lying, or standing, clench your fists, feeling confident and powerful.
2. Close your eyes and breathe however your body wants to breathe for a few moments.

- During these breaths, attempt to empty your mind and let go of any rumination.
- If you are encountering resistance, bring yourself back to your senses by noting things that you can hear, feel, or smell in this moment.
- You can also use the phrase "I wonder what my next thought will be." You'll find this helps to create space.

3. Once you find a bit of space, focus entirely on your breath as you take deep breaths in and consciously relax every inch of your body and mind as you exhale. Try to relax slightly deeper each breath you take.

4. As you are exhaling into relaxation, you will speak to yourself, either aloud or silently in your mind, saying:
   - "Everything is as it should be."
   - "I am where I need to be at this moment."
   - "There is nothing I would change about my past, as it has made me who I am today."
   - "Everything that unfolds in the future will unfold as it should."
   - "I feel completely fulfilled in life."
   - "I am completely confident in myself and our Creator."

5. **BONUS:** Think of all the people you love, silently speaking to yourself all of things you love about them. Congratulate them for the things you do not have and may be jealous of. You will only be able to do this without resistance if you feel

fulfilled. If you encounter resistance, return to the other practices.

Fulfillment is one of the more difficult emotions to allow yourself to feel on demand, especially when traveling up from deep within the lower levels. This is why it is best to make it a daily practice. As you begin to feel it more often, it will be much easier for you to feel on demand. If you are struggling to feel fulfillment with the exercise, consider the issue and ask yourself, "What would I need to do in order to feel as though nothing else needs to be done?" A crucial part of this is to do good for others on a consistent basis, but listed below are some more things that can help cultivate a feeling of fulfillment.

- **Mindfulness and Meditation:** Engage in mindfulness practices, such as meditation, deep breathing exercises, or mindful walking. These exercises cultivate present-moment awareness, reduce stress, and enhance overall well-being. This helps you to be present in the moment and obtain the peace we explored earlier in this chapter.

- **Connect with Nature:** While some people enjoy scenic walks or toughing it out in the wilderness, gardening is my suggested way to connect with nature. It requires consistent attention and will teach you many lessons about life. You will learn what is too much or not enough, and the massive effect different environments can have. That force that takes a plant from seed to stalk to fruit is the same one that keeps your heart beating. You will very quickly develop a sense of respect for and connection to it and seeing the literal fruits of your labor is sure to generate fulfillment.

**Breathe:** The simple exercise of your choice is a great way to get your heartrate up and your lungs pumping. For those that cannot or will not exercise regularly, I recommend simple breathing exercises like Wim Hof or Breathwork. There is some magic that happens when we get our blood flowing and our energy moving that generates fulfillment any time you need it.

**Help Someone in Need:** Something extraordinary happens when you help someone in need. In that simple act of kindness, a profound sense of community and belonging emerges. By extending a helping hand, you create a bond that transforms neighbors into friends and allies. You feel less alone in the world and they feel the same. The act of helping not only addresses a specific need but also fosters a deeper connection and understanding between individuals. It ignites a chain reaction of goodwill, inspiring others to lend a hand and reinforcing the fabric of a supportive and caring community.

*The 5 Levels of Conscience*

- **Pursue Your Passion Projects**: It has been years since you picked up that guitar. Or perhaps that art kit you bought months ago is still in the wrapper. Allocate time for activities or hobbies that bring you joy and fulfillment. Engaging in creative outlets away from home, such as sports, music, or any activity that ignites your passion. This will provide a sense of purpose, flow, uniqueness, and fulfillment in your life while also connecting with others by sharing your work.

- **Challenge Yourself:** When we accomplish things that we are proud of, we cannot help but step into confidence and fulfillment. We are all at different stages in our various pursuits in life. The one common thing we share in this regard is that when we are improving, we feel a deep sense of fulfillment. Set challenging but attainable goals, work to achieve them, and you will find that your entire relationship with yourself will begin to transform for the better.

- **Be a Part of Something Bigger than You**: Whether it's a sports team, hobby group, or a non-profit organization, joining a group of like-minded individuals is one of the best ways to cultivate feelings of fulfillment. Learning where you fit inside a group that is working toward a common goal will incite feelings of usefulness and uniqueness, as well as encourage a sense of community and safety. This will be multiplied if the group sets and accomplishes challenging goals. What better feeling than to achieve greatness and share the moment with those you are most connected to?

- **Embracing Novelty and Adventure**: Step outside your comfort zone and seek new experiences and adventures. Explore unfamiliar places, try new activities, or engage in novel experiences that challenge and excite you. Consider new activities like hiking, fishing, skydiving, or traveling. Bonus points if you are overcoming fears in the process. Embracing novelty and adventure gives you things to look forward to, adds new experiences for you to share with others, and cultivates a sense of accomplishment in the experience you've had during our short time on Earth.

- **Reach Out to a Friend**: Call an old friend who always makes you laugh. Reconnecting with someone who knows you well and shares your history is bound to spark laughter and joy. It can instantly uplift your spirits and bring a renewed sense of fulfillment. As you reminisce about shared memories and engage in lighthearted banter, the weight of everyday stressors fades away, replaced by a comforting feeling of warmth.

## The 5 Levels of Conscience

Remember, at the highest level of conscience, we no longer feel the desire to change anything. This opens up a safe space for us to experience the emotions of level five and the highest levels of well-being. When we feel fulfilled, we naturally and fully let go of these desires.

We feel fulfilled as we grow and empty when we are stagnant. Life in all forms is always moving, evolving, and progressing. Otherwise, it would be doomed to fail. These feelings are our Creator's way of ensuring that we never stagnate or regress as a species. We are always intrinsically motivated to grow. This growth comes from embracing new experiences, acquiring new skills, challenging ourselves, and expanding our knowledge and perspectives.

We also feel fulfilled as a result of the safety and enjoyment of the connection we experience with our community and the oneness of all Creation. This is a beautiful thing because it encourages us to join together and advance in positive directions, never stagnant or deteriorating.

Sometimes, though, fulfillment can also be found in stillness, solace, and rest. When we allow ourselves to experience moments of quiet that are not scheduled or consumed with the intake of stimuli, we open the door to new ideas, insights, and perspectives. It invites us to step away from distractions and reconnect with ourselves, fostering self-reflection and a deeper understanding of our desires and aspirations.

As fulfillment applies to the specific level four emotions, when we add it to peace, we become joyful. While peace is devoid of suffering, that does not necessarily mean it is full of joy or happiness. Fulfillment opens the door for the emptiness of peace to be filled with positive emotions. Adding fulfillment to faith creates empowerment and confidence, which turns our hope into conviction and certainty. This opens the door for us to receive the flow of Creation and perform at our highest levels because doubt and self-consciousness are no longer in our way. Finally, adding fulfillment to our compassion, we no longer feel others' pain as we help them through their suffering. Without this suffering, we are left with love. This love needs no reciprocity, nor alleviation of suffering, nor anything else to change. It just is.

Feeling more fulfilled brings about a profound transformation in various aspects of life. First, there is a noticeable shift in overall happiness and contentment. As one experiences a sense of fulfillment from their endeavors, they are more likely to wake up with a positive outlook and embrace each day with enthusiasm. This heightened sense of well-being also has a positive impact on mental health, leading to reduced stress and anxiety levels and, ultimately, better physical health. Plus, feeling fulfilled often leads to increased productivity and motivation in pursuing personal and professional goals. When we engage in activities that align with our passions and values, we are more focused, energized, and committed to our tasks, resulting in greater enjoyment.

Second, you will cultivate greater stability and confidence. You will gain more clarity on what is important to you and what is worthy of your energy and effort. This leads to increased resistance to distractions, mood swings, and the negative influence of others. In a world full of distractions and toxicity, your stability will undoubtedly attract followers in the direction you choose to embark, even if that direction is just relaxation and enjoyment of the present moment. This naturally leads to a greater sense of confidence, leadership, and empowerment.

Next, you will more find yourself more intensely engaged in the moment. Now that you've dropped the desire to change anything about reality, more of your mental space and awareness becomes fixed on the current moment. Because of this, you will notice more details about your surroundings and about others. This attention to detail is an attribute that will result in greater effectiveness and one that most people will admire about you. Where you once may have thought, "I hope this person likes me," you now notice their unique piece of clothing and compliment them which actually does make them like you more.

Lastly, you will no longer search externally for "meaning" and "purpose". Many people with a nagging sense of emptiness will ask themselves and others, "What is the purpose of life?" or "What is the meaning of life?" A very popular answer to these questions is, "To find meaning and purpose."

It is important not to romanticize the ideas of "meaning" and "purpose". We tend to get caught up in the idea that these have to be explicit and tied to a greater good in order for us to feel happy. However, these concepts are entirely man-made and subjective. Ask yourself, "What is the purpose of life for a butterfly?" Does it even matter? From an ecological perspective, their purpose is to pollinate plants. From this perspective, our purpose is to exchange oxygen for carbon and spread the seeds of fruits and sprouts of vegetables. Not so romantic, is it? Maybe this is why tending to a garden is so naturally fulfilling. Do you think a bird, or a horse asks itself, "What is the meaning of life?" What good would identifying its meaning do anyway? I can already imagine a stressed-out horse refusing to enjoy the moment with the rest of the herd.

Meaning and purpose are essentially just concepts that chain your ability to feel fulfillment to some other concept like a goal or an ambition. That helps because you always know where to find it, but when we break that chain, fulfillment can follow us wherever we go. We can find meaning in a sunset shared with loved ones, or purpose in snapping off a dead tree branch in our backyard. These concepts don't even need to be in our awareness at all. Only the idea of fulfillment in the present moment is truly relevant as we work our way towards consistent level-five awareness. Remember though, you can only feel fulfillment if you first feel acceptance, gratitude, and humility.

There are times, however, in the midst of great suffering, when our will to live and persevere can be challenged. In these times, identifying a "meaning" or "purpose" can give us something to work toward and continue to suffer for a greater good. Remember that acceptance is our first step toward fulfillment. "Meaning" or "purpose" can become the framework from which you can gather the willpower to integrate acceptance during those challenging moments of great suffering.

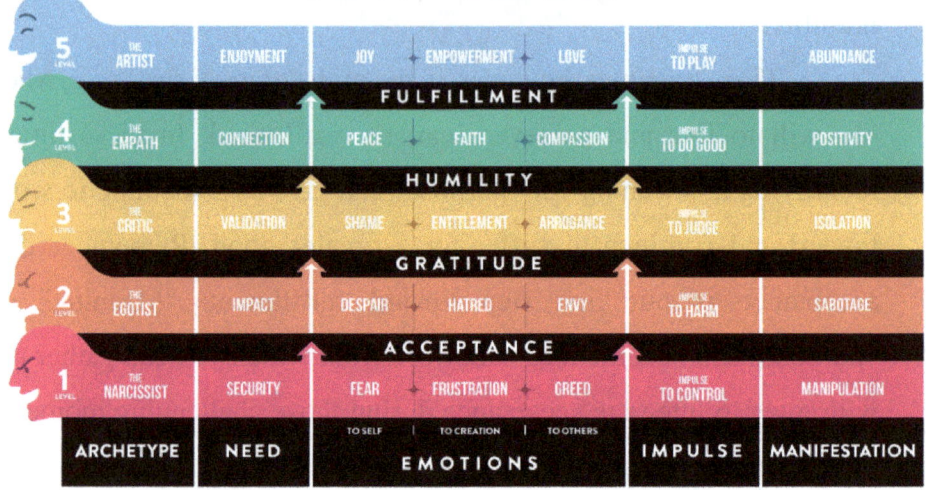

# LEVEL 5
# THE ARTIST

Born in 1918 to a royal family, Nelson Mandela witnessed the injustice of racial discrimination from an early age. In a time where dark-skinned South Africans were dispossessed of their land and had minimal political representation, Mandela enjoyed privileges that most people who looked like him would not. As the situation worsened, Mandela decided to study law and join the African National Congress in their efforts against the injustice despite the risk of arrest and imprisonment. "I learned that courage was not the absence of fear, but the triumph over it," he later went on to say.

He worked his way up the ranks of influence in the campaign against the government and, in 1964, was sentenced to life in prison. Mandela spent 27 long years in prison and, despite this tragic fate, remained grateful for the small moments. He continued his studies in secret, inspiring his fellow inmates with his faith, and in 1990, with international pressure mounting, he was released from prison. He could have easily succumbed to hatred, anger, despair, and judgment, but ultimately, he chose forgiveness and advocated for reconciliation with white South Africans instead of revenge. "Forgiveness liberates the soul. It removes fear. That is why it is such a powerful weapon," he said.

Mandela embarked on historic negotiations with then-president FW de Klerk, leading to the dismantling of the apartheid. Ultimately, Nelson Mandela was elected as South Africa's first black president in their first democratically held election.

Mandela was awarded the Nobel Peace Prize in 1993, but the greatest prize he was awarded in life was the fulfillment he felt in the justice he brought to his fellow men after decades of dedication.

## LEVEL 5 ARCHETYPE
# THE ARTIST

> **Every child is an artist. The problem is how to remain an artist once we grow up.**
> — Pablo Picasso

The archetype for level five is the artist. There are many types of art, from physical performance to music, painting to sculpture, and even comedy to tragedy. What remains constant across all types of art is the creative, playful, and passionate manner that is used to communicate an idea or emotion to the observer. Whether the artist is expressing the horrors of war or the simple beauty of a landscape, there is always a sense of fulfillment and love in the enjoyment of the work, both by the artist and by the observer. The artist does not stop creating when life offers challenges. They continue to create because that is what they are made to do. We can all aspire to live more artfully in every moment, just as our Creator presents the most perfect works of art to us everywhere we look in nature.

As we have now embraced acceptance, gratitude, humility, and fulfillment, we have finally opened ourselves to find space for the three highest emotions on the chart, which are joy, empowerment, and love. With our most pressing psychological needs satisfied, we make our way fully into the present moment with the sole intention of enjoying our experience. This encourages us to lead a playful life that inspires others to share these same positive emotions.

We can all strive to be on this level as long as we can, but we will inevitably fall to the lower levels. The beautiful thing is that the more often we spend on this level, the easier it is to find our way back. You will notice on this level, that your energy becomes childlike, not childish, and the world becomes a place where you can play and have fun in any circumstance.

## LEVEL 5 NEED: ENJOYMENT

> I don't live in the past. I just live in the enjoyment of the game.
>
> — Joe Montana

Enjoyment is the feeling of pleasure and satisfaction we get when we are engaged in something that we like or love. It releases and dissolves any tension or toxic desires and emotions we might experience in the moment. Without enjoyment, there would be no reason and no will for us to live. From the simplest things, like tasting delicious food to the pleasure of the warm sun on our skin, our enjoyment guides our behavior in certain directions. It fills us with energy and encourages us to continue those behaviors. This fuels our journey toward mastery.

If you are truly in a level-five state of conscience, your enjoyment will range from benign to altruistic. However, we do receive moments of enjoyment when we are chasing temporary pleasures and fulfilling the desires and impulses from the lower levels. Fleeting though they are, they provide the same feelings that the highest level of conscience allots to us. This is why it is so easy for us to become addicted to toxic behaviors like taking drugs. They provide quick, easy, temporary enjoyment.

While it is not easy to make it to level five, let alone learn to stay there, the benefit is that every waking moment can be permeated with the type of enjoyment that does not cause damage to self or to others. Without the distractions of toxic emotions, impulses, and desires, we are free and clear to fully appreciate the beauty of life and how everyday activities can provide us with feelings of enjoyment. You'll begin to find humor everywhere you go and use any interaction as an opportunity to spread joy and laughter.

It should be easy to recognize when you are experiencing level-five enjoyment by its lightness and clarity, but if there are any doubts in your mind, you can ask yourself:

- "Is there any desire for me to change something about this moment?"

- "Are there any harmful consequences to myself or to others by this enjoyment?"

- "Can I actively tap into acceptance, gratitude, humility, and fulfillment in this moment, or would I encounter resistance at any point?"

- "Am I being playful in this moment, or is there a sense of seriousness?"

- "After enjoying this, will I continue my impulse to play or will I sink into a lower level?"

When you are on level five, any joyful moment that harms others will not be a fully enjoyed moment. Part of our human condition is our mirror neurons and capacity for empathy that keeps our interests aligned with others. When we are not distracted by lower-level emotions, these mirror neurons will activate, and we will momentarily feel things like shame and fear as we quickly ask for forgiveness and do our best to remedy the situation. This is in stark contrast to giving in to toxic impulses that momentarily give us feelings of enjoyment as we fall right back into toxicity.

**If you carry joy in your heart, you can heal any moment.**

— Carlos Santana

## The 5 Levels of Conscience

Joy is a profound and exhilarating emotion that emerges as a deep-seated positive state of being. It is not dependent upon momentary events or material possessions and often emerges from a sense of connection and alignment with our values and passions. We feel joy because it serves a vital purpose in our lives, which is to nurture our well-being. It is a natural response to experiences and moments that align with our values and aspirations.

From an evolutionary perspective, joy reinforces positive behaviors and attitudes, encouraging us to seek activities and connections that bring us fulfillment, foster social bonds, and contribute to our overall survival and growth. It also helps to initiate biological responses that boost your immune system, improve sleep, and reduce stress, inflammation and pain. Joy also includes:

- Laughter
- Excitement
- Delight
- Bliss
- Elation
- Rapture
- Exhilaration
- Jubilation
- Ecstasy
- Gladness
- Radiance
- Contentment
- Happiness

Joy can come from accomplishing goals, being immersed in favored activities, achieving a personal or professional milestone, or seeing those achievements in others. Immersion in creative pursuits, such as painting, writing, dancing, or playing an instrument, often brings profound joy. The act of self-expression, exploring new ideas, and witnessing the tangible results of our creativity fills us with a sense of joy as well.

However, joy is not always based on what we do. We can derive joy from things we had nothing to do with at all. For example, the awe-inspiring beauty of nature has the remarkable ability to evoke a deep sense of joy within us. Witnessing a breathtaking sunset, walking through a vibrant garden, or immersing ourselves in the serenity of a forest can awaken a profound sense of joy and wonder. We can even find joy in seeing others succeed.

Furthermore, those acts of kindness, generosity, and service toward others we covered in the last chapter are also joy-invoking. Joy often springs from big moments, but it can also come from simple pleasures, so long as we hold on to the fulfillment that brought us to this level. This could be savoring a delicious meal, enjoying a peaceful walk, listening to uplifting music, or engaging in a heartfelt conversation. These seemingly ordinary moments can evoke a profound sense of joy when we fully immerse ourselves in the present and appreciate life's simple pleasures without the need to change anything.

## The 5 Levels of Conscience

You can identify joyfulness in phrases like:

- "Every day is a new opportunity for joy and gratitude."
- "I find joy in the simple pleasures of life."
- "I choose to focus on the positive aspects of any situation."
- "Being surrounded by loved ones brings me immense joy."
- "I am grateful for the beauty that surrounds me."
- "I believe that joy is contagious and strive to spread it to others."
- "Life's challenges are opportunities for growth and finding joy within."
- "I embrace moments of laughter and find joy in the company of others."
- "I appreciate the present moment and find joy in being fully present."
- "I find joy in pursuing my passions and doing what brings me fulfillment."

Joy and happiness are used almost interchangeably, but they differ in terms of their nature, duration, and underlying sources. Happiness is a broader emotional state characterized by a sense of contentment, fulfillment, and overall well-being over extended periods. Joy, on the other hand, is a more intense and profound emotion that arises in a particular moment. It can be evoked by specific moments or events that elicit a deep sense of pleasure, awe, or gratitude. The more often you leverage the tools in this book to feel joy, the more reflexive the pattern becomes and the easier it will be to return. Just as consistently living in despair will lead to depression, consistently experiencing joy will lead to long-term happiness.

# EMPOWERMENT

> *Confidence and empowerment are cousins in my opinion. Empowerment comes from within and typically it's stemmed and fostered by self-assurance. To feel empowered is to feel free and that's when people do their best work.*
>
> — Amy Jo Martin

Empowerment is a transformative and liberating concept that ignites self-belief and nurtures the realization of our true potential. It is the process of gaining control over one's life, choices, and actions while cultivating a deep sense of confidence, autonomy, and resilience. Empowerment goes beyond external validation or authority, even if it is initiated by the actions or words of others. In essence, it is an inner state of being that stems from a strong belief in ourselves and the recognition that we possess the ability to shape our own destiny. Empowerment involves developing a sense of agency, taking responsibility for our choices, and embracing the belief that we can create positive change in our lives and the lives of others, if and when we choose.

We cannot overlook the etymology of "power" inside the word empowerment. Empowerment begins with tapping into our unique power that comes with our unique strengths, talents, and capabilities. By acknowledging our strengths, we can tap into our innate potential and harness it to overcome challenges, pursue our passions, and live a life of fulfillment. We have the power to live the lives we most desire.

When we are empowered, we are able to take ownership of ourselves, including our thoughts, emotions, and actions. Empowerment involves recognizing that we have the ability to shape our responses to circumstances, even if we can't change the circumstances themselves. By accepting responsibility for our decisions and our situations, we regain control over our life's trajectory and open ourselves up to endless possibilities for growth and personal development.

We feel empowered when we feel:

- Strength
- Confidence
- Self-assurance
- Independence
- Self-determination
- Self-actualization

- Liberation
- Enfranchisement
- Encouragement
- Uplifted
- Emboldened
- Authorized
- Inspired
- Excited

When we feel empowered, we tend to align our efforts and actions more accurately with our values. We become more decisive and are filled with belief in both our ability to get the job done and the fact that what we are doing is the right thing to do at the time. It is often evident in our mannerisms. We seem to stand taller and walk with a greater sense of purpose and confidence. Our voice is also impacted by this positive emotion and we tend to be much more attractive to others, both in work and leisure. People will perceive us as having greater influence and power. We will also feel more resilient, patient, and confident in the face of obstacles. It is in these moments that we produce the most impactful work and art.

# The 5 Levels of Conscience

You may hear empowered people embody ideas like:

- "I believe in my abilities and know that I can overcome any challenge."

- "I take full responsibility for my choices and the direction of my life."

- "I trust myself to make the best decisions for my personal growth and happiness."

- "I am deserving of success, happiness, and fulfillment."

- "I embrace growth and want to learn."

- "I am not defined by my past: I am empowered to create a better future."

- "I surround myself with positive and supportive people who uplift and inspire me."

- "I choose to see setbacks as temporary obstacles on my path to success."

- "I am confident in expressing my authentic self and standing up for what I believe in."

- "I am in control of my own happiness and create a life that aligns with my values and passions."

Empowerment is an extremely positive emotion to feel, so cherish it when it comes. You will tend to achieve your goals more effortlessly and start to live a life where your talents, your passions, and your efforts align. Another significant benefit of feeling empowered is that you will see your health and overall appearance improve as well.

It is worth noting that while empowerment will help attract positive attention and circumstances from others, it will likely also attract negative attention from those who feel threatened by you. In this state, you will naturally be highly resistant to criticism, so do your best to stay compassionate towards those who try to tear you down. Take their attempts as a testament to your progress, and any situation that arises should be very easily diffused with a simple compliment or other act of generosity. Remember, we are all on our own journey and will inevitably feel similar emotions to them at some point in the future.

### LEVEL 5
### CONNECTION TO OTHERS
# LOVE

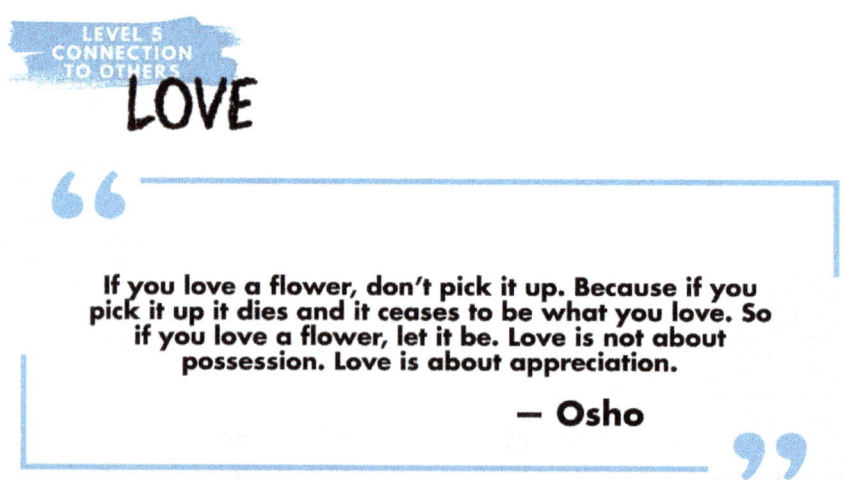

> If you love a flower, don't pick it up. Because if you pick it up it dies and it ceases to be what you love. So if you love a flower, let it be. Love is not about possession. Love is about appreciation.
>
> — Osho

## The 5 Levels of Conscience

Love is a force that transcends time, culture, and circumstance. It is an innate need that we all share as human beings. It transcends boundaries, cultures, and languages, touching the depths of our souls and reminding us of our shared humanity. Love nurtures our connections, cultivates compassion, promotes healing and growth, and brings immeasurable joy and fulfillment to our lives. By embracing love, both in giving and receiving, we tap into a profound source of strength and inspiration.

Philosophers, psychoanalysts, spiritualists, and countless others have attempted to define love. Perhaps the fact that is so hard to define explains why it is so powerful and transformative.

Love is an intricate emotion. It is a spectrum of feelings, ranging from affection and tenderness to passion and devotion. It goes beyond mere infatuation or desire, extending to a deep appreciation, acceptance, and care for others. Love serves as the foundation for meaningful connections and relationships. It cultivates a sense of belonging, acceptance, and understanding, enabling us to form intimate connections with friends, family, romantic partners, and even our local and global communities. These connections provide emotional support, companionship, and a shared sense of purpose, enhancing our well-being and enriching our lives.

Love is not possessiveness or dependence. This is greed or lust disguised as love. Instead, it is nurturing, forgiving, supportive, inclusive, and does not depend on the behavior of the beloved.

Love may also be described as:

- Affection
- Devotion
- Adoration
- Fondness
- Attachment
- Tenderness
- Caring
- Passion
- Warmth
- Endearment

No matter how you define it, most will agree that healthy love can be healing and nurturing. It provides solace during times of hardship, offering comfort, understanding, and a safe space for vulnerability. Love inspires us to embrace our authentic selves, to learn and grow from our experiences, and to become better versions of ourselves. It also inspires us to be creative and share our unique gifts and perspectives in order to foster deeper connections with others. Love also rejoices in the successes of others, giving little or no thought about ourselves. Love nourishes our souls, offering a sense of completeness and wholeness that cannot be achieved through material possessions or external achievements alone.

The power of love defies description in its ability to transform individuals and societies. It can bridge divides, break down barriers, and foster unity and harmony. Love promotes forgiveness, empathy,

## The 5 Levels of Conscience

and understanding, laying the groundwork for reconciliation and peace.

When we love or are loved, we might say:

- "I am grateful for the love and support I have in my life."
- "Being surrounded by loved ones brings me so much joy and happiness."
- "I feel a deep connection and bond with the people I care about."
- "Love gives me strength and inspires me to be the best version of myself."
- "I am blessed to have such wonderful relationships that fill my heart."
- "I cherish the moments of intimacy and closeness shared with others."
- "Love has the power to heal and mend, and I am grateful for its healing embrace."
- "The love I feel fuels my compassion and motivates me to make a positive impact."
- "I am humbled by the love I receive, and it reminds me of my inherent worthiness."

Love is very often considered a state of being as opposed to an action or feeling. This is a great perspective to have, as it reminds us that we can show love to others as a default as opposed to a reaction. This makes it easier for us to remain on level five more often. Even in conflict, it is very effective to speak lightly to yourself the words, *"I love you"* aimed toward the opposing party. This will disarm your negative instincts and remind you to stay on a higher level of conscience as you work through the issue.

It has also been said countless times throughout history that Creation exists entirely of love, and that love is the force that causes the arising of all things and of all life. When we embody this philosophy, life becomes abundantly beautiful, and it becomes much more difficult to sink to lower levels of behavior.

##  IMPULSE TO PLAY

> We don't stop playing because we grow old; we grow old because we stop playing.
>
> — George Bernard Shaw

Play is an essential and innate aspect of human nature that is not restricted by age, culture, and background. It is our expression of creativity, curiosity, and imagination that brings a sense of freedom, spontaneity, and delight. The interconnected forces of love, empowerment, and joy cultivate and nourish the impulse to play, unlocking our inner childlike spirit and enhancing our overall well-being.

First, we need love because it fosters a safe and nurturing environment where play can happen. Love provides a foundation of safety, trust, and acceptance, allowing individuals to embrace their playful impulses without fear of judgment or rejection. When we feel loved, whether through deep connections with others or self-love, we experience a sense of security that encourages exploration and uninhibited self-expression. Love also allows us to win or lose with grace and still enjoy the experience.

Then, we rely on empowerment as the fuel for play. When we feel empowered, we are more likely to embrace our playful side, as we have the confidence to take risks, try new things, think outside the box, and explore greater realms of creativity without hesitation. Empowerment enables us to break free from societal expectations and embrace our authentic selves, allowing the impulse to play to flourish. We also approach tasks with curiosity as opposed to expectation.

Then comes the joy of playfulness. Freed by love and empowerment, joy can flow uninhibited. After all, it is joy that serves as the spark that ignites the impulse to play. When we experience joy, we are naturally drawn to activities that bring us pleasure, laughter, and a sense of lightness. Joy opens the door to spontaneity, curiosity, and a childlike wonder, creating an atmosphere where play thrives.

The interplay of love, empowerment, and joy creates a powerful synergy that aligns our intentions and values with our Creator's. The benefit of obeying this impulse is that it continually feeds our overall physical and mental well-being. It promotes stress reduction, boosts creativity, enhances problem-solving skills, and cultivates a positive mindset. Playful interactions foster deeper connections and strengthen relationships, allowing for greater intimacy and understanding. It stimulates imagination, encourages self-discovery, and nurtures fulfillment and happiness.

When you reach the state where every action in your life is playful, whether it is at work, during an argument, or even while placing a simple order at a restaurant, you know you have achieved the highest level of conscience. Do your best to recognize these moments, the state of being you are in, and try to stay there as long as you are able. The more familiar you become with this state of being, the more often you can return to it.

## LEVEL 5 MANIFESTATION: ABUNDANCE

> **Not what we have, but what we enjoy, constitutes our abundance.**
>
> **— Epicurus**

Fulfilment and abundance are inextricably tied to each other. Aligning one's thoughts and actions with the energy of abundance can attract opportunities and success, but more importantly, it attracts a feeling that you already have everything you could possibly want and, therefore, any new positive aspects of life are a bonus. As you attract and experience abundance, you will naturally feel compelled to share that abundance with those around you. This could be in the form of physical gifting, creative expression, or playfully sharing joy and laughter with those around you.

At the core of manifesting abundance lies a mindset shift away from scarcity and toward the belief that Creation has limitless possibilities and opportunities. By releasing limiting beliefs and focusing on gratitude for the abundance already present in life, individuals pave the way for more blessings to flow to them and to appreciate those blessings fully.

Keep in mind that abundance does not mean the same thing to everyone. For many people, this is material wealth and possessions. To some, it will be a large family of many children. What is certain is that the more often you live on level five, the more things that truly align with your well-being will arise, align, and attract themselves to you. You will also be able to more deeply appreciate these things, as you no longer have intense desire or expectation in the way.

## LEVEL 5 PRACTICE — PLAYFULNESS

> "We are never more fully alive, more completely ourselves, or more deeply engrossed in anything than when we are playing.
>
> — Charles E. Schaefer"

Playfulness requires your undivided attention. You don't have room to think of anything else but the present moment and present action. Anything can happen at any moment, and you have to be ready! You lose your normal sense of time, and your self-consciousness tends to fade. This is the perfect scenario to encourage what people call a "flow state" or "being in the zone." In this state, your actions, your consciousness, and your task converge into one. People find that, in this state, they perform at their highest levels and have the greatest epiphanies, breakthroughs, and innovations. This is the reward you will find on level five.

There is no breathing exercise here, and no need to move anywhere from where you are at the moment. If there were an exercise, it would be laughter. The goal in level five is to stay there as long as you can and as often as you can. People and circumstances will inevitably challenge you, temporarily bringing you down into lower levels of conscience. You have the tools now to return to level five any time you are thrown off, but here are a few things you can practice on a regular basis to maintain the momentum:

- **Say yes.** Challenge yourself to engage in spontaneous activities without overthinking or planning. Say "yes" to impromptu invitations, try new hobbies on a whim, or take spontaneous trips. This is not the same as people-pleasing and lacking boundaries. It is about following the nudges of our Creator and saying yes to the fun and excitement that you may have previously rejected.

- **Dance like no one is watching**. Put some time in your schedule to be silly and carefree, doing activities that bring out your playful side. This could include playing games, dancing, painting, singing, or engaging in any creative outlet that sparks joy and allows you to express yourself freely.

- **Connect with Nature.** Nothing encourages playfulness like Mother Nature. Spend time in natural surroundings to foster a sense of awe and wonder. Take walks in the park, go hiking, or simply sit in a garden and observe the beauty of the natural world. While you are there, play with the beings around you. See if the butterfly will land on your finger. Try and feed the animals that are not dangerous. Nature has a way of rejuvenating our spirits, connecting us to our Creator, and inspiring feelings of love, joy, and empowerment.

- **Laugh often.** Seek out laughter and humor in your daily life. Watch funny movies, go to a comedy show, spend time with friends who make you laugh, or engage in activities that bring out your playful sense of humor. Laughter releases endorphins, boosts mood, and creates a positive, joy-filled atmosphere.

- **Practice self-compassion and care.** Be nice to yourself. Embrace self-love and self-empowerment by practicing self-compassion. Treat yourself with kindness, understanding, and acceptance. Celebrate your strengths. Engage in self-care activities that nourish your mind, body, and spirit, reminding yourself that you are deserving of love, joy, and empowerment. Prioritize self-care rituals that free your mind, body, and soul from worry and responsibility. This could include practices like taking a relaxing bath, practicing yoga or exercise, reading a book, or spending time in nature. Prioritizing self-care enhances overall well-being and contributes to a sense of fulfillment and balance in life.

- **Spend time on hobbies and games.** Whether you like to boat and fish, play sports with friends, paint, or play music, schedule regular time to engage in the activities you find the most enjoyable. As you consistently engage in these activities, don't be surprised if you inspire others to join you, or to start their own activities that you enjoy as well.

- **Reflect on your day.** Ask yourself, "What moments today was I playful?" Write these down and dive deeper into the way you felt in those moments. Also reflect on what may have brought you out of playfulness. This will help to identify patterns and the things that help keep you in level five.

Playfulness works wonders as a powerful catalyst for fostering creativity, building connections, and reducing stress. Engaging in playful activities triggers the release of endorphins, the brain's natural feel-good chemicals, leading to a boost in mood and overall health and well-being. When individuals allow themselves to be playful, they tap into their inner childlike curiosity. This is believed to open pathways for the highest levels of creative thinking and problem-solving.

Playfulness also enhances social interactions, breaking down barriers and fostering a positive and supportive atmosphere, whether at work or in personal relationships. People love to have fun and playfulness makes fun more available. It promotes resilience by providing a healthy outlet for stress relief, enabling individuals to approach challenges with a lighthearted and optimistic attitude. Embracing playfulness allows individuals to break free from rigid routines and adopt a more flexible and adaptive mindset.

Playfulness, in its purest sense, is completely devoid of any negativity toward the self, toward others, or toward Creation. You are entirely in the moment with only one objective: enjoyment. In this state, you are completely immune to negativity.

Embracing playfulness can lead to transformative and delightful changes in both personal and professional spheres. First, individuals can expect a heightened sense of creativity and innovation. By approaching tasks with a playful mindset, they are more likely to explore unconventional ideas and experiment fearlessly, resulting in novel solutions and breakthroughs. This is one of the ways innovations are born. Albert Einstein once said, "Creativity is intelligence having fun."

You will find that tasks you once resisted or resented are now more enjoyable. Maybe that is a chore around the house or a trip to the supermarket. Now that you are fully and playfully engaged in the moment, you can make little games about any task that will speed up time and help you get them done more enjoyably.

Playfulness also enriches relationships, as it encourages spontaneity and shared moments of joy with others. Whether it's engaging in playful banter or participating in recreational activities, being more playful strengthens bonds and nurtures a sense of camaraderie. Moreover, a playful attitude brings an element of fun and excitement to daily life, making routine tasks more enjoyable and turning mundane moments into opportunities for laughter and amusement. Expect a greater ability to cope with stress and adversity, as playfulness helps you be more optimistic and adaptable.

Playfulness has also been shown to increase the rate at which we learn. When we are playing, we are fully engaged as opposed to going through the motions. We are also enjoying what we are doing and associating positive emotions with the endeavor. The distortion of time encourages us to keep going when we otherwise might have stopped, and all of this leads to greater retention of skills and knowledge.

As with all other positive emotions and behaviors, you will be challenged. Negative circumstances will arise, and people who are operating on lower levels will feel threatened by you and try to bring you down to their level. Do your best to recognize these situations and leverage the tools within this book to enjoy your playful abundance as often as you can.

## The 5 Levels of Conscience

A WEEK IN THE LIFE

Now that we have a greater understanding of all the emotional dynamics and tools at our disposal, let's go through an example of what these may look like in everyday life.

We'll start on the drive to work Monday morning. You had a great weekend, albeit a short one as usual, and now have a long week of dreaded meetings and presentations to get through before you can relax again. You are thinking of all the things you have to do, doubting that you'll be able to get them done in time. You start to worry about the possibility of getting fired and begin to wonder, "Should I just quit? I can't stand this job anyways." You are a couple of stop signs away from arriving before you realize that you haven't been paying attention at all. As your mind was racing, your body was on autopilot, and you forgot your laptop at home. You feel a quick wave of rage rush over yourself. You think about all of the expletives you want to send your boss in the form of a resignation email, but you stop right before you act on it. You have the tools to overcome this. You park the car, breathe deep and embody acceptance. This is only a 45-minute setback in a long week. You move on to gratitude as you appreciate the stable money coming in that allows you to afford the car you are driving and home you live in. As you embrace humility you poke fun at yourself for the silly mistake as a smile begins to form. And finally, you text your boss, playfully teasing yourself. They laugh and let you know not to worry; you'll get a summary of the Monday morning meeting in your email so feel free to show up late. You masterfully navigated your first misfortune of the week.

The following afternoon coming home from work you see a new car in the driveway of your neighbor, wondering if someone is visiting. You ask your partner about it, and they say, "Oh, yeah they got a big promotion at work and bought their dream car to celebrate." You start thinking about all the hard work you've put in at your job recently, how underappreciated you are, and start to regret the career path you've chosen. You were going to hit the gym but now only feel like laying on the couch. As you head to your room to change you recognize, again, the opportunity to practice emotional mastery. You perform a gratitude practice and again appreciate the job you chose, the steady income, and reliable car you wouldn't want to trade in anyways. You've had it for years and would be driving it the same even if you were a millionaire. You move on to humility and realize, you don't know anything about the life of the neighbor. That car and promotion could be the only thing going right in their life. You decide to put on your gym clothes and head out, but not before congratulating them on their latest success. Your turn is coming; there is no doubt in your mind.

It's now Thursday and you have to sit through a meeting you've been dreading all week. It's recognition day and your quarter has not been a strong one. As they go one-by-one through all of the successes from your peers, you cycle through the shame of underachievement, and the feelings of entitlement and arrogance that say you should be the one being recognized. You aren't even a few minutes in before you remember your practice, and within seconds you are out of your head and back into the moment clapping for your peers. If they can do it, you can too. In fact, you decide to put aside a few minutes on each of their calendars to learn more about the things they are doing well. With all of that information, you are sure to bounce back next quarter.

    It's now Saturday morning and you have a jam-packed schedule. You have errands to run, gifts to buy, and meet ups to attend. You start to think to yourself, "No wonder my weekends seem so short, I hardly have a moment to myself!" You feel a sense of duty that you have to get everything done before you are allowed to enjoy yourself because that's what is good people do. You then take a couple of deep breaths and decide to try something different. You grab your partner and in a moment of spontaneity decide, it's time for a road trip. For the next day, the two of you get lost on the road with no intention other than to enjoy your free time together. On Monday, instead of waking up tired and dreadful you are energized and full of certainty that it's going to be a great week.

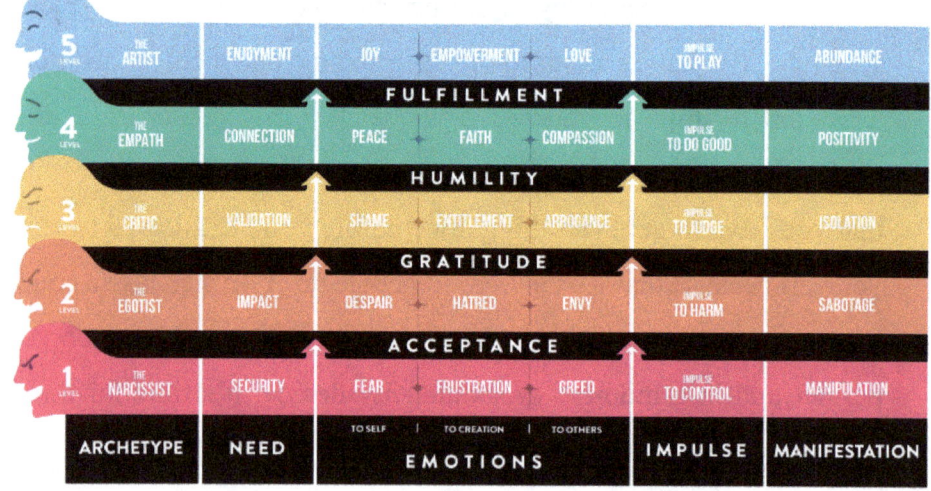

# CONCLUSION

> **Between stimulus and response, there is a space. In that space lies our freedom and power to choose our response. In our response lies our growth and freedom.**
> **— Viktor E. Frankl**

Many months after that initial interaction between my girlfriend and her cousin, there was inevitably another celebration that brought them together in the same room. My girlfriend had not forgotten how she felt the last time they were together. Not to mention the rich history of competition between them and their families. This time, though, there was something different.

She realized she didn't enjoy the tension between them. In fact, she kind of hated it. She loves her family deeply and wants what is best for all of them, including the cousin who hurt her. If she continued the same relationship dynamic, both she and her cousin would be brought down in a special moment that was meant for love and laughter. She accepted that there we many things her cousin possessed that she honestly wished that she had, and that was okay. She had so much to be grateful for, including this rare occasion that brought the family together. In this moment she decided to shift her perspective and break the cycle.

"You know, I'm really proud of you for how well you've done since we were kids. I really admire your resolve and work ethic." Her cousin couldn't believe what she'd just heard. Was she joking? Her expression was a mix of shock, relief, embarrassment, and gratitude. "Wow, that means so much coming from you. It's hard for me to admit, but I've been jealous of you since we were kids." As my girlfriend resisted the tears forming in her eyes, she started to laugh. She gave her cousin a powerful hug and went together to grab a drink from the bar as they recounted old stories and laughed at the younger version of themselves with this new perspective.

In our journey through life, as we find ourselves navigating the different levels of emotional and behavioral patterns, we don't have to feel powerless. We can smooth out these transitions while being patient with ourselves and remaining aware and present in the moment. We can shift our perspective and open our awareness to the concept that these emotions, even the most toxic ones, can be viewed as messages from our Creator. We can look at them as opportunities to incorporate new values, new ideas, and new ways of living that lead us towards joy, love, abundance, and fulfillment.

*The 5 Levels of Conscience*

Though we all oscillate between narcissism and altruism, we can empower ourselves with the tools and knowledge to shift toward altruism on a more consistent basis. This higher level of conscience moves our focus from inward to outward, cultivating positivity and abundance in our lives and the lives of those around us.

The pinnacle of our well-being lies in a state where there is no desire—no need to change anything about ourselves or our life situation. It's a state of being fully present in the world, playfully experiencing the beauty of the now, without needing change and without sacrificing our well-being or the well-being of others.

But, if we aren't in that ultimate state, we can always notice what emotional message we are receiving, and what is needed to move past it. Remember to be patient with yourself in this process. Emotions are fluid, and they have the potential to morph into one another. Give yourself time and generosity.

As you become more familiar with the framework and achieve success in implementing the exercises, I encourage you to create your own ritual that combines the four main exercises. You can do it every day in the morning when you wake up, when you shower, or any other time you have a moment to yourself. This prevents you from falling into lower levels in the first place and eliminates the need to examine which level you are on by feeling all four of the rising emotions in succession. Think of it as your daily "emotional hygiene". An example may look like this:

As you breathe deeply and exhale in relaxation, you speak to yourself: *"I fully accept this moment as a gift, with love and gratitude. I forgive myself and others for our mistakes and work humbly to fulfill my duties."*

You can also slowly go through each of the four exercises individually, in order from bottom to top when you are inevitably faced with an immediate misfortune that challenges your conscience. This is especially true when you are angry. Remember that there will always be another emotion at the root of your anger. Going through each one of the exercises in order will help create clarity for you to understand what emotion was at the root once it has subsided.

Ultimately, by incorporating this framework into our daily lives, we become more attuned to our emotions and their resolutions, enabling us to reach higher expressions of our authentic selves and attract more positive experiences in our lives and the lives of those around us. We begin to live a life that is more fulfilled and more aligned with those around us.

## FINAL WORD

After much self-reflection, research, and analysis, I've concluded that the purposes that the lower-level emotions originally served for us as a species are no longer relevant or necessary in the ways they once were. Level one helped us to survive extinction; level two compelled us to exert change into our environment; level three pulled us into cooperation; and level four refined that cooperation into competing societies that gathered resources and fostered technological innovation. In my observation, the proliferation of information serves as a turning point in our biological evolution. With the ability to understand and communicate any and all ideas in an instant and to any location, we no longer need to compete for survival. We can reach levels of understanding and cooperation that were never possible before. Wars, conflicts, and cruelty are the result of giving into emotions that do not serve our species from an objective standpoint. All the incredible effort and achievement spent toward destruction can be put toward advancement in health, well-being, and symbiosis with nature.

If we can learn to quickly release these toxic emotions and behaviors and hold each other accountable to that standard, we can shift from biological and environmental self-destruction to symbiotic self-actualization that benefits us individually and collectively without sacrifice. Those who learn to treat emotions as signals to refine our perspective, and not signals to give in to our impulses, will be the ones to lead us to this place.

It has been my great joy to share my discovery with you and I hope it enhances your life enough to share with others.

*If you enjoyed this book and think it can help others, please leave a review on the site where you purchased. That is the best way to help others find the encouragement and inspiration you received from this reading.*

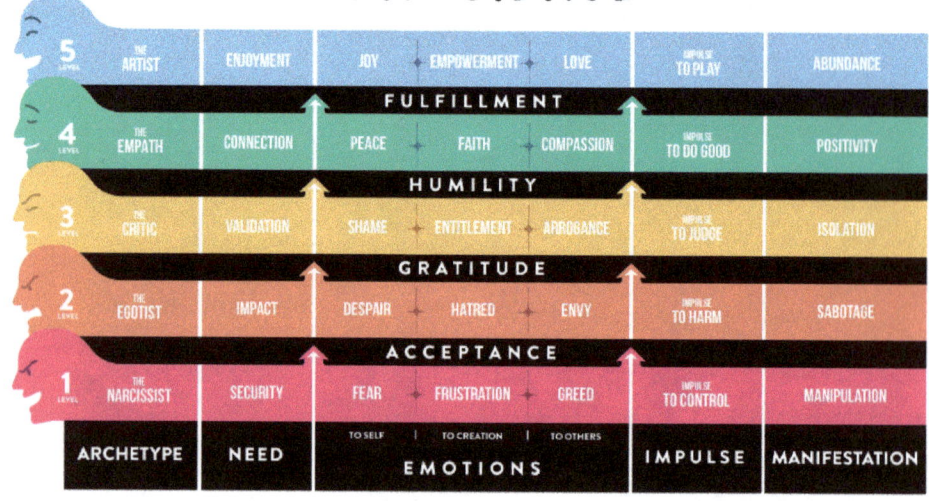

www.ingramcontent.com/pod-product-compliance
Lightning Source LLC
Chambersburg PA
CBHW060456030426
42337CB00015B/1615